# DOWNTOWN
# ITALIAN

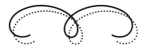

# DOWNTOWN ITALIAN

Recipes Inspired by Italy,
Created in New York's West Village

JOE CAMPANALE, GABRIEL THOMPSON,
AND KATHERINE THOMPSON

PHOTOGRAPHY BY TARA DONNE

Andrews McMeel
Publishing

Kansas City • Sydney • London

## Dedicated To Our Parents

Karen, Janey, Dawn, and Michael,
For their endless love and support

*Downtown Italian* text copyright © 2014 by Joe Campanale, Gabriel
Thompson, and Katherine Thompson. Photographs copyright © 2014
by Tara Donne. All rights reserved. Printed in China. No part of this book
may be used or reproduced in any manner whatsoever without written
permission except in the case of reprints in the context of reviews.

Andrews McMeel Publishing, LLC
an Andrews McMeel Universal company
1130 Walnut Street, Kansas City, Missouri 64106

www.andrewsmcmeel.com

14 15 16 17 18 TEN 10 9 8 7 6 5 4 3 2 1

ISBN: 978-1-4494-5034-2

Library of Congress Control Number: 2014931304

Design: Jill Bluming, The Creative Type, Inc.
Photography: Tara Donne
Food Stylist: Chris Lanier
Additional Food Styling: Patrick Decker

dellanima.com/lartusi.com/lapicio.com/anforanyc.com

ATTENTION: SCHOOLS AND BUSINESSES
Andrews McMeel books are available at quantity
discounts with bulk purchase for educational, business,
or sales promotional use. For information, please e-mail
the Andrews McMeel Special Sales Department:
specialsales@amuniversal.com.

*Downtown Italian*

# CONTENTS

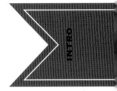

*Location*
WEST
VILLAGE,
NEW YORK

**JOE CAMPANALE:** In the fall of 2007, Katherine, Gabe, and I, along with our business partner August Cardona, opened dell'anima restaurant on 8th Avenue in New York City's historic West Village. I don't think any of us could have imagined that scenario just a few years earlier.

**KATHERINE THOMPSON:** Joe and I first met while working together at Italian Wine Merchants in Union Square, where I was the private dining chef and he was an intern. He was young, handsome, and the ultimate wine nerd, and our friendship developed over our mutual passions for food and wine. But when he called me a few years later to say that he was thinking of opening a restaurant, I thought he was crazy. When he said he wanted me to consult on the food for the establishment, I *knew* he was.

**JC:** My goal at dell'anima was to capture the feeling I'd had at my favorite neighborhood restaurant in Florence during my sophomore year abroad—a place that was warm, vibrant, cozy yet energetic, and that pushed the envelope foodwise, interpreting traditional dishes in a whole new way to make them their own.

**KT:** At the time Joe called, I had just started dating Gabe. Our relationship was brand-new and I had no idea if it was going to last, but one thing I was 100 percent sure of: Gabe's food was damn good.

**GABRIEL THOMPSON:** I had just finished working as a line cook at Del Posto, and Italian cuisine was fresh on my mind. Dell'anima was an opportunity for me to cook the food that I wanted to cook—without following any rules or regulations. So I cooked exactly what I would for myself, with an Italian twist. It was straightforward cooking with my heart and soul poured into every bite. After putting my head down and working nonstop for the first year, I suddenly realized that dell'anima had gained a following. We didn't just have regulars—we had people who ate there three to five nights a week. It was beyond rewarding. After opening our fourth restaurant, we still have the same regulars.

**JC:** Before my trip to Italy, I knew that I loved food but I couldn't imagine a career in the industry. When I returned, I couldn't think of anything other than surrounding myself with food and the people who create it. And I'm incredibly grateful that I get to do this every day. This book will share the recipes we've created in downtown New York City, an area of cobblestone streets and outdoor cafés, where the neighborhoods feel like neighborhoods, just like the little corner of Florence that I loved so much.

Whether you've been to one of our restaurants or you've never set foot in New York, I hope you'll feel when you turn these pages that you're sitting at the chef's counter, enjoying a glass of my favorite Lambrusco or a Basil Mojito (page 5), watching the action in the kitchen, and enjoying one of the amazing dishes or desserts that Gabe and Katherine have created. All of us believe in providing a warm and welcoming atmosphere, so I'd like to welcome you to this book, which captures the spirit and the flavors of our downtown New York restaurants: dell'anima, L'Artusi, L'Apicio, and Anfora.

**GT:** Believe it or not, I actually have a love/hate relationship with Italian food. I love that Italians use simple techniques and barely manipulate the ingredients. I share their passion for seasonality and local ingredients. I'm infatuated with salumi, radicchio, Parmesan, Brunello, polenta, Campari . . . But I also like to break the rules. I like pasta served with a little too much sauce. I like bold flavors: acid, salt, spice. I like taking an Italian idea and pushing it in an American direction, such as replacing the eggplant in eggplant Parmesan with green tomatoes (see page 30) or creating a chicken-fried veal Milanese (see page 136). To me, American cuisine has so many strengths in its flavors and techniques, why not incorporate them into Italian food?

At heart, I like simplicity in cooking. So my hope is that you'll find these recipes as simple and approachable as I tried to make them. In fact, my only "rules" are: Try everything—and don't be intimidated. Most of the recipes are broken down into components, many of which can be made ahead of time. Get creative—feel free to make ingredient substitutions. And taste as you go, so you'll know that every bite is going to be delicious. Because no matter what type of cuisine you're making, that's the bottom line.

**KT:** While many Italians do not consider dessert the highlight of the meal, I like to challenge that concept! There is nothing I enjoy more than seeing someone fall in love with a dessert I've made. Instant gratification is the biggest highlight of my job. Of course, this can be a challenge when my food follows Gabe's—who can resist eating that extra bite or two of pasta and then being too full for dessert (a practice I'm guilty of all the time)? The advantage of this book is that you can cook what you want, when you want. In the mood for savory comfort food? Try Gabe's amazing Gnocchi with Braised Chicken (page 83), the ultimate chicken and dumplings. Want something sweet and homey, yet sophisticated? Dive into my Bittersweet Chocolate Budino (page 168) or Brown-Butter Tart with Sour Plums (page 189).

I hope you'll be inspired to try all of these dishes, from the simplest to the most complex (although, honestly, nothing in this book is terribly complicated—Gabe and I like to eat, too, and we don't want to wait all day for it, either!). You may discover, as we have, that it's okay not to be 100 percent "authentic" all the time. The point is to work with great ingredients, treat them right, cook with love, and create something you and everyone else wants to eat right that minute. Have fun!

Just like our restaurants, this book is a team effort. It showcases our individual roles in the restaurants, and the friendship that's been forged there. We're excited to share our recipes with you. The drinks and dishes in these pages have been inspired by Italy, informed by downtown New York City, and crafted with our own personal touch. They're our kind of Italian: downtown Italian.

—*Joe Campanale, Katherine Thompson,*
*Gabe Thompson*

# NOTES ON WINE

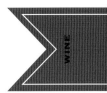

The study of Italian wines could be a lifelong pursuit. With more than 1,000 unique indigenous grapes; 20 political regions, all of which produce wine; and a range of climates from Alpine in the north to desert in the south, there is more diversity and more opportunity to have a truly local experience with wine in Italy than anywhere in the world.

Italy makes a lot of wine—only France produces more each year—and the U.S. is Italy's largest export market. So it's amazing to think that not much more than a generation ago, Italy's wine industry was nearly in ruins. Most wine was not bottled at the winery; instead it was shipped to cities and bottled for domestic consumption or made by large, industrial producers selling huge amounts of anonymous wine. A winemaker's job was neither esteemed nor lucrative.

Fortunately, times change. Italy's new prosperity and the worldwide embrace of the Mediterranean diet (which, let's be serious, is Italian cooking) have created a new mindset among the country's producers. Thanks to world-class winemakers who have trained at the best schools—or, even better, learned from the traditions of their families—and to vintners who are rediscovering old, forgotten grapes and re-creating traditional winemaking methods, there has never been such an abundance of high-quality Italian wine.

To help make sense of all the options, I like to analyze wine from four different perspectives—region, grape, producer, and wine style. This overview should give you a framework for the delicious "puzzle" that is Italy and its wines.

*—Joe Campanale*

*Region*   If sunshine, a temperate climate, hillside vineyards, and unique soils are required to make great wine, Italy has those in abundance.

Italy is a 750-mile peninsula, with the Adriatic Sea to the east and the Tyrrhenian Sea to the west, and plenty of rivers and lakes that contribute to the temperate climate. Along the northern border, the Alps and Dolomites act as a rain and wind shield, creating the perfect climate for winemaking on their south-facing hillside vineyards. The wines from these vineyards are ripe thanks to abundant daytime sunshine but stay very balanced because of the cooling winds that come off the mountains at night.

There is more vintage variation in the north because of this "marginal" climate; in the warmer south, the vintages are a lot more consistent from year to year. However, many northern producers tell me that due to climate change they are seeing a lot more consistency than in their parents' winemaking years.

A range of lower-altitude mountains, the Apennines, runs down the spine of Italy from Liguria near the border of France to the "toe" of Calabria. In fact, more than two-thirds of Italy's land is either hilly or mountainous, and most of the country's high-quality winemaking takes place on those hillsides, where the soils tend to be poor with good drainage.

The importance of soil in winemaking cannot be overstated. Soil has physiological effects on grapes depending on whether it's compact or loose, has good or poor drainage, and is cool like clay or absorbs heat like slate. It also has biological effects, providing grapevines with nutrients and water. Counterintuitively, poor soils make great wine: When soils don't hold water or nutrients, the vines are forced to dig deep to find water and food. The result is a hardy vine producing flavorful fruit. From the extraordinary white calcareous (calcium-rich) soils in Piedmont and Tuscany to the black volcanic soils on Mount Etna and in Campania and the red iron-rich soils in Friuli, Italy has the best worst soils!

But the most Italian wine tradition of all is to drink what's local. With that in mind, at L'Apicio I added a variety of American wines to our list, starting with those most local to the restaurant: the wines of Long Island and upstate New York. Long Island has a climate similar to Bordeaux and growers like Shinn Estate Vineyards, Macari, and Paumanok on the North Fork are making unique and sometimes beautiful wines in both white and red. Channing Daughters Winery on the South Fork is pushing the envelope with wines from some obscure grape varieties such as Italian Tocai Friulano and Austrian Blaufränkisch. In the Finger Lakes, Riesling is king and producers like Hermann J. Wiemer, Bloomer Creek, Dr. Konstantin Frank, and Keuka Lake Vineyards make some of the most exciting examples in the world. When I order from Keuka Lake, Mel Goldman drives his station wagon downstate to deliver my wine. That's local.

*Grape*   Unlike, say, Chardonnay grapes, which are now grown around the world and produce wines that taste different in each place (Chardonnay from Napa Valley will be ripe and buttery; one from Burgundy will have bright acidity and minerality), many of Italy's more than 1,000 native grapes are found exclusively in their regions. And the producers I like best strive to make wines that beautifully represent those regions. Our wine list at dell'anima celebrates this diversity and this connection to Italy's past and present. Here are a few of our favorites.

## WHITES

**PIGATO AND VERMENTINO (LIGURIA):** These coastal grapes, and the wines they create, have a salty minerality that comes from growing so close to the water.

**VERDICCHIO (MARCHE):** Made from grapes on Italy's east coast, these wines can be very light and refreshing.

**FRIULANO AND RIBOLLA GIALLA (FRIULI):** These two grapes produce outstanding wines in a variety of styles: fresh and crisp, full and rich, even orange (see Wine Style, page xiii).

**FIANO AND FALANGHINA (CAMPANIA):** Grown in high-altitude volcanic soils, these grapes make mineral-rich wines with honeyed notes.

## REDS

**NEBBIOLO (PIEDMONT AND LOMBARDY):** Nebbiolo is not only Italy's greatest grape, it's one of the best in the world. Wines have mouth-drying tannins, mouthwatering acidity, and earthy complexity.

**SANGIOVESE (TUSCANY):** Italy's other great grape grows throughout central Italy but finds its most expressive examples in Tuscany. Sangiovese tends to have cherry and tobacco notes with great acidity. Whether simple Chiantis or complex Brunello di Montalcinos, these are some of the best food wines.

**SAGRANTINO (UMBRIA):** This dark, tannic yet floral grape is grown in small quantities, but almost all of it is high quality. It takes years to reveal its stunning perfume.

**NERELLO MASCALESE (SICILY):** This is the grape of Europe's tallest active volcano, Mount Etna. It creates wines that feature some of Nebbiolo's earthiness and Pinot Noir's perfume, with a smokiness that can only come from growing up on an active volcano.

**AGLIANICO (CAMPANIA AND BASILICATA):** This deep purple wine is smoky from the regions' volcanic soils and very dry, but it can be extremely complex and delicious.

*Producer*  Finding a few producers you like and who are dedicated to their craft is a more reliable method of discovering wines you love than any other factor. One of the best ways to find value wines (especially at the higher end) is to choose an off-vintage wine from a good producer. The vintage is the year in which the grapes were harvested; but in reality, it is the summation of all of the winemaker's vineyard work and all the weather up to the harvest. Off-vintage wines are those made in years that wine critics agree were not top quality for winemaking in that area. But an off-vintage wine from a good producer will still be a good wine; it will just cost less.

At our wine bar, Anfora, we have chosen a small handful of producers we like and offer many wines from each of them. These producers take good care of their land (using no harmful chemicals) and their grapes (they do not alter their nature in the winery). Producers featured on all our lists include Occhipinti, Paolo Bea, Bartolo Mascarello, Fontodi, and Venica & Venica.

*Wine Style*  I think the thing that keeps most people from drinking wine they love is a reluctance to use the vocabulary that would get them there. If you know how much you want to spend, if you want sparkling, white, rosé, or red (or maybe orange), and if you can use a few words to describe the style you like, chances are you'll find a wine that pleases you. The final part of the equation is finding a wine store or restaurant with a good selection and knowledgeable staff.

## SPARKLING

**DRY:** Little to no sugar

**OFF-DRY:** Some sugar

**SWEET:** Noticeable sweetness

**COLOR:** Pale white, golden (aged wines), rosé, or red, like my favorite, Lambrusco

**PÉTILLANT NATUREL** ("pet-nat," as the cool kids say): We love this old style of sparkling-wine making. These lightly sparkling wines often come from producers who make wine in a very natural way. They're also a great value.

## WHITES

**LIGHT, FRESH, CRISP:** Generally unoaked young wines that are very refreshing and have good acidity

**FLORAL, AROMATIC, EXOTIC:** These have flavors that jump out of the glass.

**FULL, RICH, ROUND:** Weighty, riper wines; they can be oak-aged or not.

**ORANGE WINES:** We love these. These are white wines that are made with skin contact the way a red wine would be produced. They are golden in color and dry like a red, and they are versatile in accompanying food.

## REDS

**LIGHT IN COLOR BUT FULL OF FLAVOR:** These tend to be soft and aromatic. Sometimes these reds are good chilled.

**DRY, TEXTURED:** Great food wines. The tannin that causes the dryness is exactly what you need for protein.

**FULL, DEEP, DARK:** These are rich, dense wines. They're too taxing on the palate to drink by themselves but a bit of food balances them out.

In the Antipasti, Primi, and Secondi chapters, I suggest a beverage pairing with each recipe—mostly wine recommendations, sometimes beer. In each case, I recommend a style that complements the ingredients in the dish (e.g., "an off-dry Riesling"), followed by a particular brand or producer that we feature at the restaurants. If your wine shop doesn't carry that brand, just ask for something in the same style.

*Chapter 1*

# APERITIVI

It's 6:00 p.m. in Italy and *aperitivo* is in full force. In Milan, the bars are filled with stylish people sipping cocktails as fashionable as the clothes they're wearing. In Florence, students sit on the banks of the Arno with bright red Negronis, nibbling on cheese and colorful crostini. In Udine, a bustling little city in the foothills of the Alps, fluorescent Aperol spritzes abound in the piazzas.

Italians have a long tradition of starting their meal with a bitter drink to inspire hunger *(aperitivo)* and closing their meal with a stronger drink to settle the stomach *(digestivo)*. These drinks are low in alcohol, so that by the time dinner comes, they're feeling good, not drunk.

I was first introduced to *aperitivo* culture when studying in Florence as a college student. I'd be heading home from school as the local watering holes were filling up, and when I peeked in, I realized that if you bought a drink, you could eat as you pleased from platters of tasty-looking bites. Needless to say, that was immensely appealing to a student on a limited budget who desperately wanted to know everything about Italian food and culture.

This chapter will introduce you to some of our favorite *aperitivi* and to the drinks at our restaurants that were inspired by this Italian cultural phenomenon. The great thing about *aperitivo* cocktails is that they are easy to make at home; they don't require a ton of prep, cleanup, or special equipment; and they are so uniquely, authentically Italian. Once you get to know the ingredients, you can experiment and come up with some great flavor combinations of your own. Following are just a few things to keep in mind—and then a word about the classics.

—*Joe Campanale*

**BALANCE IS THE KEY TO A GREAT DRINK.** Bitterness and acidity balance sweetness; sweetness and temperature balance alcohol (the sweeter and colder a drink is, the smoother the taste of the alcohol).

**USE ONLY FRESH CITRUS.** Squeeze the fruit the day you're going to use it, preferably right before making the drink. Citrus juices lose their zing quickly. Never use store-bought, pre-squeezed lemon or lime juice from a container.

**USE LARGE ICE CUBES.** The idea is to minimize surface area to avoid watering down drinks. Silicone ice cube trays come in a variety of sizes and release cubes easily.

**CHILL YOUR GLASSWARE.** This keeps your drinks cold and prevents ice from melting. Keep your glasses in the refrigerator, or fill the glasses with ice water while you're building your drink.

**PICK YOUR EQUIPMENT.** Use a two-piece cocktail shaker (pint glass for mixing plus metal tin for shaking), an unpainted wood or plastic muddler, a serrated paring knife, and a plastic cutting board. I also like the tall, thin Japanese jiggers available at cocktailkingdom.com.

**CHOOSE YOUR BRANDS.** There are no substitutes for the iconic Italian aperitifs, but you can use any of your favorite spirits (vodka, gin, rum, etc.).

## BAR SET UP

- COCKTAIL SHAKER
- MUDDLER
- COCKTAIL MEASURE (JIGGER)
- BAR SPOON
- STRAINER
- PARING KNIFE
- CUTTING BOARD

---

**CAMPARI:** In Italy, nothing screams "cocktail hour" like the sight of this bright-red liqueur with the singular bitter/sweet taste, developed by Gaspare Campari in 1860.

Campari was originally served straight, on the rocks, or with soda water, and always with a wedge of orange. At Gaspare's bar, Caffè Campari, he served it with sweet red vermouth and soda water. Because the drink was popular with American G.I.s stationed in Italy, it became known as the "Americano." In Florence several years later, the gregarious Count Negroni ordered his Americanos with gin instead of soda water. Today the Negroni cocktail is synonymous with *aperitivo* hour.

# NEGRONI

Ice

1½ ounces Campari

1½ ounces red vermouth

1½ ounces gin (London Dry style)

Strip of orange peel, for garnish

Fill a mixing glass with ice. Add the Campari, vermouth, and gin. Stir with a bar spoon until the glass feels very cold. Strain into a chilled cocktail glass. Garnish with the orange peel. Serves 1.

**APEROL (APP-ER-ALL):** I like to describe Aperol as Campari's sweet little sister. Although it has the same sugar content as Campari, its relative lack of bittering ingredients and lower alcohol content means that it feels softer and more approachable. The main ingredients are bitter orange, gentian root, rhubarb, and cinchona—all typical of Italian aperitifs, but here blended in perfect proportions to make an extremely balanced beverage.

While traveling through the Friuli region, I was surprised to notice that around *aperitivo* time, Campari was shunned and the iridescent orange Aperol was everywhere. I took a sip of one as the sun was setting over the Julian Alps and was hooked. It was the most refreshing drink I'd ever had, simultaneously quenching thirst and inducing hunger.

# APEROL SPRITZ

| | |
|---|---|
| Ice | 1 ounce sparkling wine (such as Prosecco) |
| 2 ounces Aperol | |
| 1 ounce soda water | Wedge of orange, for garnish |

Fill a wineglass with ice. Add the Aperol, followed by the soda and sparkling wine. Garnish with the orange wedge. Serves 1.

**NOTE:** People will argue about the correct proportion of sparkling wine or soda water, or whether you should only use one or the other. I like a combination of both.

**CYNAR (CHEE-NAR):** Of the three most popular Italian aperitifs, Cynar—with its excellent balance of slight sweetness and alluring bitterness—is the one I crave the most. I've noticed it also has the most digestive qualities of any aperitif, so if I have a big meal coming, I always grab the Cynar.

Cynar is made with 13 herbs and roots, one of them being *Cynara scolymus*—artichoke—but don't worry, it doesn't taste anything like artichokes. At 16.5% alcohol, it falls somewhere between Campari and Aperol, and it is enjoyed throughout Europe on the rocks or with soda (the Swiss like it with orange juice). In the past five years, the popularity of Cynar has really taken off in New York, where bartenders love it for its deep bitterness without the astringency found in many *amari* (bitter liqueurs). It's also an easy substitute for red vermouth in cocktails and it pairs well with a variety of liquors. Unlike Campari and Aperol, Cynar doesn't star in many classic cocktail recipes, so I recommend trying to create your own. I like to drink my Cynar with soda and a squeeze of lemon, which I feel balances out its slightly syrupy quality.

# CYNARINO

| | |
|---|---|
| Ice | Soda water |
| 2 ounces Cynar | Wedge of lemon, for garnish |
| 1 ounce freshly squeezed lemon juice | |

Fill a rocks glass with ice. Add the Cynar and lemon juice. Stir. Top with soda and garnish with the lemon wedge. Serves 1.

**VERMOUTH:** Vermouth is a form of flavored or aromatized wine that was extremely important in the cities of northern Italy in the 18th and 19th centuries and remains an ingredient in many classic cocktails today. Vermouth must be flavored with wormwood, which gives it a dry/bitter flavor.

When we opened dell'anima in 2007, the selection of available vermouths left a lot to be desired; there were only a couple of dry French white vermouths, such as Noilly Prat, and some sweet red Italian ones like Cinzano and Martini & Rossi. When we were lucky we snagged a bottle of the limited-supply Carpano Antica Formula, which claimed to be the original recipe for vermouth and dated back to the late 1700s. Today there are tons of vermouths available from all over the world, and even some great domestic examples. The rule used to be that red vermouth was Italian and sweet, while white vermouth was French and dry, but now there's a wide variety of styles. Not only are these great in classic cocktails like the Manhattan and Negroni, but they're fantastic on the rocks with a slice or peel of orange.

Vermouth is a perishable product—when it is opened it begins to oxidize, like a bottle of wine. To improve its life span, cap it as soon as it's used and put it in the refrigerator. I like to buy half bottles of vermouth, just to make sure the bottle doesn't go off before I've finished using it.

Now that we've laid a foundation with the classic aperitivi, there's all kinds of fun we can have with new variations, as you'll see on the following pages.

# BASIL MOJITO

Basil is quintessentially Italian, but it also reminds me so much of summer in New York. The aroma and flavor of this bright green herb create a delicious, more savory version of the classic Mojito.

ROCKS GLASS

APERITIVI

## SERVES 1

3 to 4 fresh basil leaves, plus more for garnish

2 teaspoons sugar

¾ ounce freshly squeezed lime juice

2 ounces El Dorado 3 Year Old Rum (or your favorite white rum)

Dash of citrus bitters

Ice

Soda water

Add 3 to 4 basil leaves to a rocks glass. If they are big, tear them once or twice. Add the sugar and lime juice. Muddle gently. Add the rum and bitters; stir. Add ice. Top with soda water. Garnish with basil leaves.

# ROASTED-ORANGE NEGRONI SBAGLIATO

This cocktail was inspired by the sparkling bright-red drink I discovered while studying in Italy. The Negroni Sbagliato ("broken" or "mistaken" Negroni, because it features sparkling wine instead of gin) was inexpensive, and it quickly became my favorite drink.

ROCKS GLASS

## SERVES 1

1 wedge roasted
orange (see Notes)

1 ounce red vermouth
(such as Carpano
Antica Formula)

1¼ ounces Campari

Ice

1¼ ounces Lini
Lambrusco Bianco,
or other sparkling
white wine

Orange peel,
for garnish

Place the orange wedge in a mixing glass and add the vermouth. Muddle the two so that the charred bits of the orange are released into the vermouth. Add the Campari and ice; cover and shake.

Fill a chilled rocks glass with ice. Strain the contents of the mixing glass into the rocks glass. Add the sparkling wine. Do not stir, as this will dissipate the bubbles. Garnish with the orange peel.

**NOTES: Roasted orange:** To roast the orange, first cut it into 8 wedges and soak the wedges in red vermouth overnight. Roast them on a hot grill until they are charred and caramelized on both sides. You can keep them refrigerated, covered with red vermouth, for 1 week.

**Preparation:** This cocktail can also be made as a regular Roasted-Orange Negroni by using gin instead of sparkling wine (in the same proportions) and stirring with ice instead of shaking; strain into a chilled cocktail glass. Never shake the drink with the sparkling wine; the mixing glass will "explode" like a can of soda after being shaken.

# WHITE NEGRONI

Cocchi Americano is one of my favorite aperitifs; it tastes like a strong but slightly sweet white wine with a bit of flat tonic. Served on the rocks, it is extremely refreshing—great for a summer gathering outdoors. For this recipe, I put a bunch of things in a glass on a whim, including Luxardo Maraschino, a Marasca cherry–flavored liqueur. Somehow it all tasted delicious together on the first try.

ROCKS GLASS

## SERVES 1

2 ounces Cocchi Americano

1 ounce American-style gin (such as Bluecoat)

½ ounce Luxardo Maraschino

4 drops grapefruit bitters

Ice

Extra-long strip of orange peel, for garnish

In a mixing glass, stir together the Cocchi, gin, Luxardo Maraschino, and bitters with ice. Fill a chilled rocks glass with fresh ice. Strain the mixture into the rocks glass. Garnish with the orange peel.

# SANDIA DEL FUEGO

Sandia del Fuego is the summer drink of Anfora. It is spicy, a little sweet, and—if you choose to use mescal instead of tequila—smoky. I made this drink for Chef Tim Love's Burgers 4 Babies charity event in Fort Worth, Texas. Something told me that Texans would like a spicy tequila drink, and I was right. Everyone kept calling it a watermelon margarita, but I didn't care—they were drinking them and coming back for more.

COCKTAIL
GLASS

APERITIVI

## SERVES 1

3 to 5 cubes chile-infused watermelon (infusion is optional; see Notes)

1¾ ounces blanco tequila

¾ ounce freshly squeezed lime juice

½ ounce agave simple syrup (see Notes)

Ice

Place the watermelon cubes in a mixing glass and add the tequila, lime juice, and simple syrup. Add ice, cover, and shake vigorously. Strain into a chilled cocktail glass (for a perfectly smooth drink, double-strain through 2 strainers).

**NOTES: Watermelon:** To infuse the watermelon, place the cubed watermelon in an airtight container. Fill the container with tequila and 6 chiles (such as Thai chiles or fresh jalapeños). Cover and refrigerate for 24 hours, or until the watermelon is as spicy as you like. Drain and discard the chiles.

**Agave simple syrup:** Combine 2 parts agave syrup and 1 part water in a small saucepan and cook over medium heat until completely combined. Let cool. You can also make this with sugar or honey, but agave is a natural partner for the tequila (they come from the same plant). Kept refrigerated in an airtight container, this simple syrup will last for at least 1 month.

# BLAME IT ON THE APEROL

In order to pass the time while working in the cellar at Anfora, I sometimes start singing corny songs about what's stored in the wine room. One day I picked up a bottle of one of my favorite aperitifs and blurted out "Blame it on Ah-ah-hah-ah-Aperol!" Now I had to come up with a drink; the name was just too good. I started with the classic Aperol Spritz, left out the sparkling water, and added a good dose of gin.

LARGE
WINEGLASS

APERITIVI

**SERVES 1**

Ice

1 ounce Aperol

1 ounce American-
style gin (such as
Bluecoat; see Note)

¼ ounce freshly
squeezed
lemon juice

3 ounces sparkling
white wine (such
as Prosecco)

Slice of orange,
for garnish

Fill a wineglass with ice. Add the Aperol, gin, and lemon juice; stir. Top with the sparkling wine and garnish with the orange slice.

**NOTE:** Bluecoat American Dry Gin is a good American-style gin, which has more floral notes than London Dry style. Bluecoat is produced locally, in Philadelphia, and is very reasonably priced, so I like it for all those reasons. But feel free to substitute your own favorite American-style gin.

# TEXAS MIMOSA

One day I was having cocktails with my friend Tim Love, chef-owner of The Lonesome Dove Western Bistro and Woodshed Smokehouse in Fort Worth, Texas. At the time, I was racking my brain trying to think of new drinks for the brunch service we were about to debut at L'Artusi. Tim mentioned that down in Texas he loves to drink tequila with fresh grapefruit juice, and I thought that would make a killer mimosa. Today it is our most popular brunch cocktail. It's a great year-round drink, but it's especially good in the middle of the winter when grapefruit is at its best.

CHAMPAGNE FLUTE

## SERVES 1

4 ounces dry sparkling white wine

2 ounces freshly squeezed grapefruit juice

1 ounce blanco tequila (such as Partida Tequila Blanco)

½ ounce simple syrup (see Note)

2 dashes grapefruit bitters

Long strip of grapefruit peel, for garnish

Pour the sparkling wine, then the grapefruit juice, tequila, simple syrup, and bitters into a flute. Stir lightly. Garnish with the grapefruit peel.

**NOTE:** To make the simple syrup, heat equal parts sugar and water in a small saucepan over medium heat, stirring until the sugar is dissolved. Let it cool. It will last at least a month in an airtight container in the refrigerator. It's extremely versatile—you can use it in coffee, iced tea, or any drink that needs sweetening. It's also easy to infuse with flavor using a vanilla bean, herbs, or spices; just strain the simple syrup before stirring it.

# LUCA MANO FREDDO

Katherine and Gabe have the most beautiful little boy, Luke. His name comes from both Katherine's love for Paul Newman *(Cool Hand Luke)* and Gabe's love of *Star Wars* (Luke Skywalker). We joked about how great "Cool Hand Luke" sounds in Italian—"Luca Mano Freddo"—and decided a name like that needed its own cocktail. I wanted to use one of my favorite ingredients, Velvet Falernum; it's derived from sugarcane, and I use it to sweeten cocktails and give them extra complexity and spice. I knew this drink had to be served in a julep cup—because, of course, your hand should get super cool.

JULEP CUP

**SERVES 1**

6 small pieces of cucumber, plus wedge of cucumber, for garnish

5 leaves fresh mint, plus sprig of mint, for garnish

¾ ounce Velvet Falernum (see Note)

Ice

2¼ ounces dill-infused vodka

¾ ounce freshly squeezed lime juice

Muddle the cucumber pieces and mint leaves with the Velvet Falernum in a julep cup. Add ice. Top with the vodka and lime juice; stir. Garnish with the sprig of mint and wedge of cucumber.

**NOTE:** Velvet Falernum is not always easy to find. You can substitute regular or vanilla-infused simple syrup instead.

# NIKO

This cocktail is a staff favorite at Anfora. We love the Nikolaihof winery in Austria and were excited to create a drink that showcases their elderflower syrup. The syrup pairs very well with American gin, which favors floral and citrus notes over spice and herbal flavors. This is a great drink to make in large batches; just top everyone off with the sparkling wine at the end.

CHAMPAGNE
FLUTE

APERITIVI

## SERVES 1

¾ ounce American-style gin (such as Bluecoat)

¾ ounce Nikolaihof elderflower syrup (see Note)

3 dashes of orange bitters

Sparkling wine, for topping

Long strip of orange peel, for garnish

Pour the gin, elderflower syrup, and bitters into a Champagne flute. Stir with a bar spoon. Top with sparkling wine. Garnish with the orange peel.

**NOTE:** If you can't find Nikolaihof elderflower syrup, this drink is also delicious with St. Germain.

# BLUEBERRY BOURBON SMASH

This recipe originated at an event hosted by my buddy Rachael Ray. I was asked to create a summertime cocktail featuring bourbon, so I made an icy drink using fresh, local blueberries and sweetened it with a honey simple syrup. The recipe is nice and easy—it doesn't even need a garnish, as the bits of blueberry create their own—so you can make several of them quickly. Taste your blueberries before making the drink: If they're not very sweet, add a little more simple syrup.

ROCKS GLASS

APERITIVI

## SERVES 1

8 blueberries

2 ounces bourbon (such as Jefferson's)

¾ ounce freshly squeezed lemon juice

¾ ounce honey simple syrup (see Note)

Ice

Place the blueberries in a mixing glass and add the bourbon. Muddle to release the juice and peels from the blueberries. Add the lemon juice, simple syrup, and ice. Cover and shake vigorously for 30 seconds. Pour the complete contents, including the ice, into a rocks glass.

**NOTE:** To make the honey simple syrup, heat equal parts honey and water in a saucepan over medium heat, stirring until completely combined. Let cool. It will last for several months in an airtight container in the refrigerator.

# DIRTY SPICY MARTINI

Although I'm not a huge fan, Gabe and Katherine love dirty martinis (with olives and a splash of olive juice). I wanted to create one that would satisfy them *and* me, so I decided to try using the brining juice from the B&G pickled peppers we all love. The martini was so good, even I approved. I garnish this with a big red pickled pepper. It's dramatic, but it's also a warning that you have a serious drink coming!

COCKTAIL GLASS

**SERVES 1**

2¼ ounces American-style gin (such as Bluecoat) or vodka

¾ ounce Cinzano white vermouth

2 dashes of celery bitters (such as Fee Brothers; see Notes)

2 bar spoons juice from 1 jar of B&G pickled peppers (see Notes)

Ice

1 B&G pickled pepper, for garnish

Combine the gin, vermouth, bitters, and B&G juice in a mixing glass. Add ice and stir. Strain into a chilled cocktail glass. Garnish with the pickled pepper.

**NOTES: Bitters:** If you can't find celery bitters, you can use regular bitters instead, or leave them out altogether.

**Pepper juice:** The pepper juice is spicy, so feel free to use more or less according to your taste.

# MONTENEGRO FLIP

Despite its frothy, fun appearance, this is actually a sophisticated bitter drink, meant to be sipped slowly. I love how egg whites give roundness and creamy texture to a cocktail that nothing else can replicate. It's important to use the freshest farm eggs you can find.

ROCKS GLASS

**SERVES 1**

1½ ounces Amaro
   Montenegro

¾ ounce freshly
   squeezed
   lemon juice

½ ounce Bittermens
   Amère Nouvelle

½ ounce egg
   white (less than
   1 egg white)

Ice

3 dashes Angostura
   bitters

Twist of orange
   peel, for garnish

Pour the Amaro Montenegro, lemon juice, Amère Nouvelle, and egg white into a cocktail shaker and shake without ice for 15 seconds. Add ice and shake for another 30 seconds. Pour into a neat glass or rocks glass and top with the Angostura bitters. Garnish with the orange twist.

# AMARENA CRUSH

This was one of the original drinks on our list when we opened dell'anima. I wanted to create a drink that would appeal to a lot of people while being easy to produce on what we hoped would be busy nights. This one—the perfect mix of sweet and sour, balanced and approachable—hits the mark.

COCKTAIL
GLASS

APERITIVI

### SERVES 1

6 amarena cherries (or Luxardo Maraschino cherries; see Note)

2 ounces vodka

¾ ounce Luxardo Maraschino liqueur

¾ ounce freshly squeezed lemon juice

Ice

In a mixing glass, muddle 5 of the cherries with the vodka. Add the Maraschino and lemon juice. Add the ice; cover and shake. Strain into a chilled cocktail glass. Garnish with the remaining cherry.

**NOTE:** I love amarena sour cherries from Italy, but the drink is also great with Luxardo brand cherries (use one fewer than called for, as they tend to be large). In the summer, try this drink with fresh cherries from the market.

# NARDINI SOUR

This drink re-creates a Pisco Sour—the famous Peruvian drink featuring pisco (brandy) and bitters—using Italian ingredients. The closest thing to pisco in Italy is grappa, which is made with pomace, the grape skins, seeds, and pulp left behind after the juice is extracted for wine. What makes this drink so successful is the beautiful foamy texture, thanks to the egg white, and the dramatic pour of Nardini Amaro that we do tableside—the brown amaro contrasts beautifully with the white cocktail.

COCKTAIL
GLASS

## SERVES 1

1½ ounces Nardini
   Bianca Grappa

1 egg white (see Note)

1 ounce simple syrup
   (see page 12)

¾ ounce freshly
   squeezed
   lemon juice

Ice

Nardini Amaro,
   for garnish

Pour the grappa, egg white, simple syrup, and lemon juice into a mixing glass. Cover and shake without any ice for 30 seconds. Add the ice and shake again for 30 seconds. Pour into a chilled cocktail glass. Garnish with a drizzle of Nardini Amaro.

**NOTE:** Be sure to use absolutely fresh eggs.

# FARMER'S FRIEND

A few years ago, Gabe and Katherine took a trip to Italy and came back raving about the Brachetto they drank in Piedmont—a slightly sparkling, lightly sweet, pale red wine. Once spring hit and there was something at the New York farmers' market besides root vegetables, I was eager to create a drink using the Brachetto and the first ingredients of the season. Then I gave it a little mojito twist using Flor de Caña, the Nicaraguan rum.

ROCKS GLASS

**SERVES 1**

1 teaspoon finely chopped rhubarb, plus stalk of rhubarb, for garnish

½ ounce simple syrup (see page 12)

4 fresh mint leaves, plus sprig of mint, for garnish

¾ ounce freshly squeezed lime juice

Ice

2 ounces Flor de Caña rum

2 ounces Brachetto d'Acqui

Place the chopped rhubarb in a rocks glass and add the simple syrup, mint leaves, and lime juice. Smash the rhubarb and mint with a muddler. Fill the glass with ice. Add the rum and stir. Top with the Brachetto. Garnish with the rhubarb stalk and mint sprig.

# THE GILLILAND

Through the years we've become close friends with many of our regulars, perhaps none more so than Eric Gilliland, a screenwriter, comedian, professional bingo caller, and whistle savant—in other words, a quintessential West Village character. Eric's favorite drink is the Manhattan (whiskey, sweet red vermouth, and bitters), and in his honor I created a new riff using Rittenhouse Rye, Bonal (a French aperitif flavored with quinine and gentian, a wildflower), and barrel-aged bitters. It is a Manhattan, but even more quirky and lovable, like Eric himself.

COCKTAIL
GLASS

APERITIVI

**SERVES 1**

3 ounces rye whiskey
(see Note)

¾ ounce Bonal

2 dashes of barrel-
aged bitters (such
as Fee Brothers)

Ice

1 amarena cherry,
for garnish

Pour the rye, Bonal, and bitters into a mixing glass. Fill with ice and stir. Strain into a chilled cocktail glass. Garnish with the cherry.

**NOTE:** There's no need to use an expensive fancy rye in this drink; its subtle nuances will be lost. We use Rittenhouse Rye; Old Overholt would also be a good choice.

# TORINO SOUR

This cocktail is unabashedly based on the New York Sour. As a layered cocktail it is very impressive-looking, but in reality it has few ingredients and is very easy to make. You can serve it up or on the rocks.

COCKTAIL
GLASS

## SERVES 1

1¾ ounces rye whiskey (such as Michter's rye)

1 ounce freshly squeezed lemon juice

¾ ounce honey simple syrup (see page 17)

½ ounce Nonino Amaro (or your favorite amaro)

Ice

½ ounce Italian red wine

In a cocktail shaker, shake the rye whiskey, lemon juice, simple syrup, and amaro with ice. Strain into a chilled cocktail glass or over ice. Slowly pour the red wine over the back of a bar spoon into the glass.

## Chapter 2
# ANTIPASTI

My interpretation of the first course in an Italian meal is not at all Italian. Traditionally this course features bite-sized foods, served cold or at room temperature—sliced cured meats, olives, or pickled vegetables. All of these ingredients are delicious, but to me they seem more appropriate in a bar setting than in a dining room.

I wanted antipasti dishes that were thoughtfully composed, so I sought out unusual ingredients that inspired me, such as octopus and sweetbreads. I took non-Italian ingredients such as avocados and treated them the way an Italian cook would: simply seasoned and dressed with olive oil and lemon. I paired contrasting textures and flavors: soft with crunchy; raw with roasted; spicy and sweet.

And, of course, my personal preferences show up in all of the antipasti dishes at our restaurants. I like food that is generously seasoned. If a dish needs black pepper, I add a few more turns from the grinder than usual. I have a love affair with acid and always opt for an extra squeeze of lemon juice. If I can make a dish spicy, I don't hesitate. Italians don't typically season their dishes this way, but that is how I think food should be served.

I should note the abundance of salad recipes in this chapter. When Katherine and I visited Italy recently, we could not find salad anywhere, which was such a disappointment. I'm obsessed with salads. When I was a young cook, I would dream up restaurant menus in which the salad category dominated the page. The various tastes and textures from salad greens are always an inspiration. I can't get enough of radicchio, escarole, and butter lettuce. And salads are always fun to dress up. My go-to formula is to use a healthy amount of dressing (heavy on the vinegar), add a spectacular cheese, and crunch it up with croutons or nuts. It is a no-fail combination. Plus, salads are a beautiful way to showcase gorgeous seasonal ingredients from the farmers' market, especially in summer. To me, a delicious salad is the best way to start off an Italian meal, even if it is unconventional.

Of course, I make Joe's life very difficult. Almost all of the ingredients I love in these recipes—chiles, lemon, even asparagus—are the hardest to pair with wine. Yet Joe gladly accepts the challenge and always nails the pairing. Be sure to heed his suggestions.

—Gabriel Thompson

# GREEN TOMATO PARMESAN

Green tomatoes are among those ingredients that I always wanted to work with, but I could never think of anything besides Southern-style fried green tomatoes. One day, it occurred to me to serve fried green tomatoes as I would eggplant Parmesan—and it worked. The green tomatoes pair well with the ripe ones in the sauce, and they add a tanginess to this dish that does not exist in eggplants. This take on eggplant Parmesan is unlike anything you will find in Little Italy.

*Pair with*
CHILLED SANGIOVESE OR ORGANIC BEAUJOLAIS

Tomatoes have a lot of acidity; you need acid in the wine so the dish doesn't clobber your drink. We like: Fontodi Chianti Classico or Jean-Paul Brun Beaujolais "L'Ancien."

**SERVES 4**

3 tablespoons extra-virgin olive oil

3 to 4 tablespoons chopped fresh basil

1 tablespoon plus 1 teaspoon minced garlic (about 4 garlic cloves, minced)

¼ teaspoon red chili flakes

Kosher salt

2 cups (16 ounces) canned crushed Italian tomatoes, with juice

3 medium green tomatoes (about 12 ounces total)

½ cup unbleached all-purpose flour

3 large eggs

1 cup panko breadcrumbs

Olive oil, for frying

8 ounces mozzarella cheese, sliced ¼ inch thick

¼ cup grated Parmesan cheese

3 fresh basil leaves, torn

To make the tomato sauce, heat the extra-virgin olive oil, basil, garlic, chili flakes, and a generous pinch of salt in a small to medium saucepan over medium heat. Sauté for 2 to 3 minutes, until aromatic. Before the garlic turns brown, add the crushed tomatoes and another pinch of salt. Bring to a boil. Decrease the heat to low and simmer for 5 to 10 minutes until thickened. Remove from the heat. Taste and add more salt, if necessary.

Remove the core from each green tomato. Thinly slice off and discard the very top and very bottom of each tomato. Cut each tomato into 4 (⅓- to ½-inch-thick) slices.

Place the flour, eggs, and breadcrumbs in 3 separate shallow bowls. Gently whisk the eggs. Season each tomato slice on both sides with kosher salt. One at a time, press each tomato slice into the flour on both sides. Then dip both sides into the egg mixture, then into the breadcrumbs. Place on a baking sheet.

Pour enough olive oil into a large sauté pan to reach a depth of ½ inch. Heat the oil over high heat. When the oil is hot, turn down the heat to medium. Working in batches, gently place the battered green tomato slices in the oil. Cook until golden brown on each side, 2 to 3 minutes per side.

Preheat the broiler to high. Place the cooked slices of green tomatoes on a baking sheet. Top each slice with ½ tablespoon of the tomato sauce and spread the sauce evenly over the slice. Break the mozzarella slices into 12 pieces, about ½ ounce each. Place a piece of mozzarella on top of each slice of tomato and sprinkle each slice with 1 teaspoon of the grated Parmesan.

Place the tomato slices under the broiler. Cook until the cheese has melted and looks golden brown, 4 to 5 minutes. Be sure to rotate the pan and check the tomatoes frequently so that the cheese does not burn.

To serve, rewarm the tomato sauce, if desired. Spread 1 to 2 tablespoons of tomato sauce onto each serving plate. Distribute the tomato slices decoratively onto each plate, 3 slices per plate. Garnish with the torn basil leaves and serve.

ANTIPASTI

# GRILLED BRUSCHETTA

Bruschetta served with toppings on the side is a fixture on dell'anima's menu: Everyone loves the idea of creating their own bruschetta by combining different toppings and varying the amount on each. Don't hesitate to dollop tomatoes on the avocados or slather the lily confit on every bite.

*Pair with*
A LIGHTLY SPARKLING WHITE WINE

This will work with all of the bruschetta toppings. We like: Lini 910 "Labrusca" Lambrusco Bianco NV.

**SERVES 4 TO 6**

Beefsteak Tomatoes with Basil (recipe follows)

Avocados, Lemon, and Pepper (recipe follows)

Lily Confit (recipe follows)

1 large Italian-style baguette

1 head of garlic, cloves separated, skins removed

½ cup extra-virgin olive oil

Prepare your toppings of choice, then preheat a grill to medium-high. Cut the baguette into 1-inch-thick slices. Grill each slice of bread for a few minutes per side, or until grill marks appear. Rub raw garlic over one side of each piece of hot bread. Drizzle with the olive oil. Serve warm alongside the bruschetta toppings.

Alternatively, use a toaster, toaster oven, grill pan, or broiler to toast the bread until the edges are golden brown with slightly burnt bits.

## BEEFSTEAK TOMATOES WITH BASIL

This is a classic bruschetta topping—with a little hit of spice, because I can't help myself.

**SERVES 4 TO 6**

3 medium-sized beefsteak tomatoes (about 1 pound), diced

¼ cup freshly torn basil leaves

2 tablespoons extra-virgin olive oil

1 garlic clove, minced

Kosher salt

Pinch of red chili flakes

Toss together the tomatoes, basil leaves, olive oil, and garlic. Season generously with salt and add the red chili flakes. The topping can be prepared a few hours in advance and kept at room temperature, but is best served the day you make it.

## GRILLED BRUSCHETTA
**CONTINUED**

## AVOCADOS, LEMON, AND PEPPER

Think of this as a streamlined, Italian-style guacamole—like a Vespa compared to a Harley-Davidson.

**SERVES 4 TO 6**

2 avocados

1 tablespoon freshly
squeezed lemon juice,
plus more to taste

2 teaspoons extra-
virgin olive oil

1 teaspoon kosher salt

8 turns freshly cracked
black pepper

Slice the avocados in half and remove the pits. Scoop the avocado flesh into a medium bowl and mash with a fork. Add the lemon juice and olive oil. Stir together and season with the salt and pepper. Add more lemon juice to taste. Serve immediately.

## LILY CONFIT

The flowering bulbs of garlic, shallots, and onions (allium) are all related to the lily family; "confit" means that the lily bulbs slowly cook in olive oil, taking on a beautiful golden color and a melt-in-your-mouth texture. To peel the garlic, shallots, and onions quickly, put them all in a large bowl and pour hot water over them. Let them sit for a minute, and the skins will peel off easily.

**SERVES 4 TO 6**

1 cup plus 2 tablespoons
extra-virgin olive oil,
plus more as needed

½ cup halved garlic cloves
(halved lengthwise)

½ cup medium dice shallots

½ cup quartered
cipollini onions

½ cup halved pearl onions

½ teaspoon kosher salt

2 B&G hot pickled
peppers, stems and
seeds removed, julienned
(about ¼ cup)

Preheat the oven to 350°F. Heat the 2 tablespoons olive oil over medium heat in a medium (3-quart) ovenproof saucepan. Add the garlic, shallots, cipollini onions, pearl onions, and salt. Sauté until the onions begin to sweat, but do not take on any color, 5 to 10 minutes. Add the pickled peppers. Cover the onion mixture with the 1 cup olive oil. Add more olive oil if necessary to cover the onions. Cover the pan with aluminum foil or a lid. Bake for 1 hour, or until the onions are very soft.

Remove the cover and let cool to room temperature. Serve the confit and oil with bruschetta. The confit can be made ahead and stored in the refrigerator for several days. Bring to room temperature before serving.

# CHARRED OCTOPUS WITH CHICORIES, CANNELLINI BEANS, AND CHORIZO

Octopus seems to be the go-to chef ingredient for most restaurants in Manhattan, and for good reason: Properly prepared, octopus is absolutely delicious. In dell'anima's first year, we hosted a New Year's Eve tasting dinner, and this dish was the hit of the night. I collaborated with my chef friend Chris Frazier to concoct a combination of octopus, beans, chorizo, and chicories. To this day, it is our most popular dish at dell'anima.

*Pair with*
A FULL-BODIED ROSÉ

Choose one that will stand up to the flavorful, meaty octopus. We like: Montenidoli Canaiuolo.

## SERVES 4

- 4 ounces dried cannellini beans
- 7 cups water, plus more for soaking the beans overnight
- ½ Spanish onion, cut into 4 pieces
- 1 medium carrot, peeled and sliced into 1-inch-thick pieces
- 1 celery stalk, cut into 1-inch-thick pieces

- 1 garlic clove
- 1 bay leaf
- 1 tablespoon kosher salt, plus more for seasoning
- Braised Octopus (recipe follows)
- ¼ cup extra-virgin olive oil
- 2 tablespoons julienned or small dice Spanish chorizo

- 1 teaspoon thinly sliced lemon zest
- 1 teaspoon fresh oregano leaves
- Pinch of red chili flakes
- 1 tablespoon freshly squeezed lemon juice
- 3 ounces chicories (any combination of torn radicchio leaves, endive spears, and/or frisée leaves)

To cook the cannellini beans, soak the beans overnight in an abundant amount of water. Discard the water and rinse the beans. Place the rinsed beans in a medium (3-quart) saucepan. Add the water, onion, carrot, celery, garlic, and bay leaf. Bring to a boil over high heat. Decrease the heat to low. The liquid should be just under a simmer. Cook until the beans are tender, about 2 hours. Approximately 15 minutes before the beans are cooked, add the 1 tablespoon kosher salt. Taste the bean cooking water and make sure it tastes seasoned. Add more salt if necessary.

When the beans are done, remove the pan from the heat and let the beans cool to room temperature. Discard the vegetables and aromatics. If you are not using the beans immediately, the beans can be stored in their cooking liquid, covered, in the refrigerator for several days.

Using a slotted spoon, scoop out 1 cup of the cooked beans. Add as much of the bean cooking liquid as will fit in the cup measure. Set aside.

## CHARRED OCTOPUS WITH CHICORIES, CANNELLINI BEANS, AND CHORIZO
**CONTINUED**

To cook the braised octopus, place a large cast-iron skillet over high heat. Add 2 tablespoons of the olive oil. Season the octopus pieces generously on all sides with salt. When the oil is hot, carefully add the octopus pieces to the skillet. Place a saucepan or other heavy-duty pan on top of the octopus to weigh it down in the skillet. Cook the octopus pieces undisturbed until golden brown and charred on the bottom, 2 to 4 minutes. Remove the weight and gently turn over the octopus pieces with tongs in order to cook the other side. Place the weight on top of the octopus pieces. Cook the other side for another 3 to 4 minutes. The octopus should be evenly charred on both sides. Remove the octopus from the hot pan and set aside.

Heat a large sauté pan over high heat. Add 1 tablespoon of the olive oil, the chorizo, lemon zest, oregano leaves, and chili flakes. Sauté for 2 to 3 minutes. Add the reserved cup of beans with its liquid to the pan. Cook until the bean liquid reduces by half, 2 to 3 minutes. Add the remaining 1 tablespoon olive oil, the lemon juice, chicories, and charred octopus. Toss together to combine. The chicories will wilt just slightly.

To serve, divide the mixture among serving plates. Be sure to equally divide the octopus, 2 tentacles per serving. Make sure each plate gets a piece of octopus head. (The head tastes like octopus bacon!) Serve immediately.


## BRAISED OCTOPUS

**MAKES JUST UNDER 1 POUND**

1 (approximately 2-pound) octopus (if previously frozen, make sure it is completely thawed; see Note)

1 (750 ml) bottle of dry red wine

1 Spanish onion, cut into 8 pieces

1 medium carrot, peeled and sliced into 1-inch-thick pieces

1 celery stalk, cut into 1-inch-thick pieces

2 tablespoons kosher salt

1 teaspoon black peppercorns

1 bay leaf

1 lemon

½ orange

Place the octopus, wine, onion, carrot, celery, salt, peppercorns, and bay leaf in a large Dutch oven. Cut the lemon and orange in half and remove the seeds. Squeeze the citrus juice on top of the octopus and add the lemon and orange halves to the cooking liquid. Add enough water to completely submerge the ingredients in the Dutch oven.

Bring the mixture to a boil over high heat. Decrease the heat to low. The liquid should remain just under a simmer. Place a small sauté pan over the floating octopus in order to submerge the octopus in the cooking liquid. Poach the octopus for 2 to 2½ hours, until the tentacles tear easily from the head of the octopus. The tentacles will be tender and firm (not mushy).

Remove the octopus from the poaching liquid. Let sit at room temperature until cool enough to handle. Place the octopus under cold running water in the sink. Using your hands, gently remove and discard the slimy, dark outer layer from the octopus. Discard the octopus beak, or mouth, located on the head of the octopus where all of the tentacles meet. Separate the 8 tentacles from the head. Cut the head into 4 pieces.

The cooked octopus can be stored airtight in the refrigerator for 3 to 4 days before proceeding with the recipe.

**NOTE:** Octopus can be found at specialty food stores such as Citarella in New York and at seafood stores. At our restaurants, we order from Octopus Garden in Brooklyn, 718-946-1100.

ANTIPASTI

# ROASTED CHERRY TOMATO SOUP WITH CARAMELIZED ONION– PECORINO CROSTINI

This happy accident is a hyped-up version of grilled cheese with tomato soup. One day we had an abundant amount of roasted cherry tomatoes with no plan in sight. I decided to puree the tomatoes and it ended up becoming the best-tasting tomato soup I've ever had. Paired with caramelized onions and pecorino, this is a great first course or lunch. Be sure to crack a ton of black pepper onto the crostini—tomato and black pepper is a great match.

*Pair with*
SPARKLING
ROSÉ

The effervescence offers a nice contrast to the soup, and the flavors complement it. We like: Scarpetta Timido.

## SERVES 4

- 3 pints cherry tomatoes
- 6 garlic cloves
- 8 sprigs fresh thyme
- ¼ cup extra-virgin olive oil, plus more for garnish

- 1¼ teaspoons plus ½ teaspoon kosher salt, plus more for seasoning
- Freshly cracked black pepper
- ¼ cup water

- 2 teaspoons (or more) red wine vinegar
- ½ teaspoon sugar
- Caramelized Onion– Pecorino Crostini (recipe follows; for serving)

Preheat the oven to 425°F. In a large bowl, toss together the cherry tomatoes with the garlic, thyme, the ¼ cup olive oil, the 1¼ teaspoons salt, and a few turns of pepper. Spread the mixture out onto a baking sheet. Roast until the tomatoes are slightly golden in color, 20 to 25 minutes.

Remove the garlic cloves and thyme sprigs. Puree the tomatoes and any pan juices in a blender until smooth. Add the water, vinegar, sugar, and the 1 teaspoon salt; blend to combine. Taste and adjust the seasoning as needed.

Warm the soup in a small saucepan. Divide among bowls and garnish each with a drizzle of olive oil. Serve with the crostini.

# CARAMELIZED ONION–PECORINO CROSTINI

These crostini are also delicious served alongside a salad; or present them by themselves as hors d'oeuvres.

**MAKES 8 CROSTINI**

1 tablespoon extra-virgin olive oil, plus more for drizzling

1 tablespoon unsalted butter

1 large red onion, thinly sliced

1 bay leaf

2 sprigs fresh thyme

¼ teaspoon kosher salt

½ cup dry white wine (such as Pinot Grigio)

8 (½-inch-thick) slices of crusty white baguette, sliced on the diagonal

¼ cup grated Pecorino Romano

Freshly cracked black pepper

In a large sauté pan, heat the 1 tablespoon olive oil and the butter over medium heat. Add the onion, bay leaf, and thyme sprigs. Cook, stirring occasionally, until the onion is slightly golden in color, 20 to 25 minutes. Season with the salt. Add the wine and cook until the liquid evaporates, 6 to 7 minutes. Continue cooking the onion until caramelized (it should be dark amber), 8 to 10 minutes longer. Remove from the heat and discard the bay leaf and thyme sprigs.

Preheat the oven to 350°F. Drizzle a baking sheet with a little olive oil. Arrange the slices of bread on the baking sheet. Distribute the onion evenly over the bread slices. Sprinkle each slice with ½ tablespoon of the Pecorino and season with pepper. Bake until the bread is toasted and the cheese is melted, 15 to 20 minutes.

# ESCAROLE WITH BAGNA CAUDA DRESSING AND PARMESAN

In northern Italy, crudités are traditionally served with a warm anchovy-garlic dip called *bagna cauda*. We turned the dip into a salad dressing and created an Italian version of Caesar salad. I'm not always a fan of anchovies, but when used correctly, they add incredible depth of flavor. In this salad you will not taste fishiness, but instead a complex saltiness, and the escarole is sweeter than expected. If you are feeling especially indulgent, make the Roasted Mushrooms with Bacon and Eggs (page 55) and serve it on top of this salad. It is the perfect one-dish meal.

*Pair with*
A CRISP
WHITE

A white with light effervescence is refreshing with the dressing. We like: Ameztoi Txakoli from Spain.

**SERVES 4 TO 6**

### ESCAROLE

1 head of escarole, tough outer leaves removed and discarded

### CROUTONS

2 cups ½-inch cubes country bread

1½ tablespoons extra-virgin olive oil

¼ teaspoon kosher salt

8 turns freshly cracked black pepper

### BAGNA CAUDA

1½ anchovy fillets with backbones, packed in salt (about 1½ ounces; see Notes)

¼ cup fresh oregano leaves

¼ cup coarsely chopped fresh flat-leaf parsley

1 head of garlic, cloves separated, skins removed

¾ cup extra-virgin olive oil

⅛ teaspoon red chili flakes

### DRESSING AND ASSEMBLY

1 tablespoon bagna cauda

2 tablespoons extra-virgin olive oil

¼ cup freshly squeezed lemon juice

Kosher salt and freshly cracked black pepper

2 ounces Parmesan cheese

To prepare the escarole, separate the inner leaves and thoroughly wash in several changes of cold water. Spin dry. Chop the leaves crosswise into 1-inch-wide strips. Set aside in the refrigerator until ready to dress.

To make the croutons, preheat the oven to 350°F. Toss the bread cubes with the olive oil and salt; season with the black pepper. Spread the bread cubes out onto a baking sheet and bake until golden brown and crispy, 10 to 15 minutes. Remove from the oven and set aside to cool. These can be made ahead and stored at room temperature in an airtight container.

Meanwhile start the *bagna cauda* by soaking the anchovies in 2 cups of cold water for 30 minutes. Drain. Using a paring knife or your hands, gently remove the backbones from the anchovy fillets. Rinse the fillets under cold water. Place the anchovies in a small saucepan. Add the oregano, parsley, garlic, olive oil, and chili flakes. Bring to a simmer over medium-low heat. Cover the pan and decrease the heat to low. Slowly simmer the mixture for approximately 45 minutes. Stir occasionally to make sure that none of the ingredients stick to the bottom of the pan.

Strain the anchovy/garlic mixture, reserving the anchovy oil. In a blender, puree the anchovy/garlic mixture with 2 tablespoons of the anchovy oil. Discard any remaining anchovy oil. The *bagna cauda* will keep for 4 to 5 days in an airtight container in the refrigerator; or freeze it in ice cube trays.

To make the dressing and assemble, stir together the 1 tablespoon *bagna cauda* mixture with the olive oil and lemon juice. Reserve the remaining *bagna cauda* for another use (see Notes).

Place the escarole in a salad bowl. Drizzle the dressing over the escarole, season with salt and a generous amount of freshly cracked pepper, and toss together. Add the croutons and grate some of the Parmesan over the salad. Toss together and garnish with more freshly grated Parmesan.

**NOTES: Anchovies:** Salt-packed anchovies can be found in Italian specialty stores, such as Buon Italia in New York (buonitalia.com). We use Agostino Recca brand. The flesh is firmer, sweeter, and meatier than that of standard anchovies sold at grocery stores. Packed in salt, the anchovies will last a lifetime refrigerated. If they are unavailable, you can use 1½ ounces of oil-packed anchovies instead; there's no need to soak them.

*Bagna cauda:* You can use the extra *bagna cauda* dressing to create anchovy-scented croutons—toss bread cubes in the dressing, then toast them. Or create a quick *puttanesca* pasta by adding a small amount of *bagna cauda* to a simple tomato sauce with olives.

# BUTTER LETTUCE WITH LEMON CREMA, OLIVES, TOASTED HAZELNUTS, AND GORGONZOLA

Despite the cream, this dressing is surprisingly light and refreshing. It's also very easy to make—just don't stir it so vigorously that you whip the cream, as one of my prep cooks once did. When combining the lemon juice and cream, stir the mixture as you would stir cream into your coffee: very gently. Feel free to be dramatic with the presentation. Butter lettuce leaves have a beautiful shape and structure, and when stacked together, they form a spectacular tower.

*Pair with*
A SOUR BEER

Pick one with acidic and creamy notes to complement the creamy, nutty, tangy dish. We like: Petrus Aged Pale Ale.

## SERVES 4 TO 6

⅓ cup heavy cream

2½ tablespoons freshly squeezed lemon juice

1 teaspoon finely grated lemon zest

1½ tablespoons minced shallots

¼ teaspoon kosher salt

¼ teaspoon freshly cracked black pepper

1 head butter lettuce, leaves separated and thoroughly washed

½ cup pitted and coarsely chopped Kalamata or Alfonso olives

½ cup toasted and coarsely chopped hazelnuts

4 ounces Gorgonzola Piccante cheese, chilled (see Note)

In a small bowl, gently stir together the cream, lemon juice, lemon zest, shallots, salt, and pepper. In a large bowl, use your hands to toss together the lettuce leaves, olives, and hazelnuts. Toss the greens with the lemon cream dressing using your hands: It's the best way to handle the floppy lettuce leaves and to make sure everything is evenly coated. Adjust the seasonings as needed, keeping in mind that the Gorgonzola will be salty.

Layer 3 to 4 lettuce leaves, combining large and small leaves, onto each serving plate, scattering the nuts and olives between the layers.

Grate some Gorgonzola on top of each salad. If the Gorgonzola is difficult to grate, place it in the freezer for a minute or two to solidify the cheese.

**NOTE:** Gorgonzola Piccante is an aged Gorgonzola that is firmer and easier to grate than the younger Gorgonzola Dolce.

# ROASTED CARROT, AVOCADO, AND WATERCRESS SALAD

The roasted carrots in this salad take on a dried-fruit sweetness and chewy texture that play well against the pasta-like strips of raw carrots. The dressing is super tart and assertive, but it is balanced well with the creamy cumin yogurt. I have a fondness for cumin that stems from my upbringing on Tex-Mex food. Even though it's not at all Italian, I always try to find a home for cumin in at least one dish at all of my restaurants.

*Pair with*
A MARGARITA!

2 ounces white tequila (Richard Betts' Astral), ¾ ounce Luxardo Triplum Triple Sec Orange Liqueur, ¼ ounce agave simple syrup (optional), pinch of salt. Shake hard; strain over ice.

**SERVES 4 TO 6**

## ROASTED CARROTS

10 medium carrots (about 1¼ pounds), peeled and sliced on the diagonal into ½-inch to 1-inch pieces (about 3 cups sliced carrots)

2 tablespoons extra-virgin olive oil

2 teaspoons honey

½ teaspoon salt

## SHALLOT DRESSING

2 tablespoons minced shallots

¼ cup extra-virgin olive oil

¼ cup red wine vinegar

1 teaspoon kosher salt

Freshly cracked black pepper

## CUMIN-YOGURT DRESSING

½ teaspoon cumin seeds

½ cup Greek yogurt

2 tablespoons extra-virgin olive oil

½ teaspoon kosher salt

## SALAD

1 bunch watercress

2 medium carrots, peeled

½ cup roughly chopped toasted pistachios

1 avocado, diced

To make the roasted carrots, preheat the oven to 350°F. In a medium bowl, toss together the carrots, olive oil, honey, and salt. Spread the carrots onto a baking sheet. Roast in the oven until fork-tender and slightly golden brown, about 45 minutes. Remove from the oven and set aside.

To make the shallot dressing, stir together the shallots, oil, vinegar, salt, and pepper in a small bowl. Be sure to season with a generous amount of black pepper. Set aside.

To make the cumin-yogurt dressing, lightly toast the cumin seeds in a small sauté pan over medium heat until aromatic, 2 to 3 minutes. Grind the seeds finely in a clean spice grinder. Stir together the yogurt, olive oil, salt, and cumin. Set aside.

To make the salad, clean the watercress and discard the large stems and any wilted leaves. Place the watercress in a large bowl.

Use a vegetable peeler to shave long, thin carrot strips from the raw carrots. Turn the carrots as the strips are removed (you'll have a little core left that you can toss).

Add the raw carrot strips, pistachios, avocado, and roasted carrots to the watercress. Toss together with half of the shallot dressing. Feel free to add more dressing if the salad seems too dry. Taste and adjust the seasoning as needed.

Divide the cumin-yogurt dressing among serving plates. Use a spoon to create a thin layer of yogurt over the bottom of each plate. Divide the salad among the plates on top of the yogurt. Serve immediately.

# HEIRLOOM TOMATO AND WATERMELON PANZANELLA SALAD WITH BLACK PEPPER BACON AND PICKLED WATERMELON RIND

Panzanella salad is a classic Tuscan dish made with tomatoes and stale bread. In order to showcase summer produce, why not include watermelon? I've also made versions of this dish with peaches, plums, and other stone fruits. And as we all know, everything tastes better with bacon. In fact, this salad could be considered a cross between panzanella and a deconstructed BLT sandwich.

*Pair with*
A GOOD ROSÉ
WITH SOME
SYRAH

Rosé and watermelon is a match made in heaven, and the addition of Syrah will complement the bacon and tomato. We like: Copain Wines.

**SERVES 4**

- ½ cup diced watermelon rind (outer green rind removed; inner white rind cut into ¼-inch dice)
- ¾ cup champagne vinegar
- 1½ tablespoons sugar
- 1½ tablespoons water
- ¼ teaspoon kosher salt, plus more for seasoning
- 4 slices thick-cut bacon
- Freshly cracked black pepper
- 1½ cups ½-inch cubes Italian bread
- 3½ tablespoons extra-virgin olive oil
- 1½ cups 1-inch cubes seedless watermelon
- 4 heirloom tomatoes, quartered
- 1 cup cherry tomatoes, halved
- ¼ cup thinly sliced red onion (about ½ small red onion)
- 6 fresh basil leaves, torn
- Freshly squeezed juice of 1 lemon (about 2 tablespoons)

Place the watermelon rind in a small heatproof bowl. In a small saucepan bring the champagne vinegar, sugar, water, and ¼ teaspoon salt to a boil. Pour over the watermelon rind, and let sit for at least 30 minutes, uncovered. The pickled watermelon rind can be made ahead. Store, covered, in the refrigerator. Before serving, drain off the liquid.

Preheat the oven to 350°F. Lay the bacon out on a baking sheet and season generously with black pepper. Bake until the bacon reaches the desired crispness, 20 to 30 minutes. Drain on paper towels. Maintain the oven temperature.

Toss the bread in 1½ tablespoons of the olive oil. Generously season with salt and pepper. Arrange on a baking sheet and toast in the oven until golden, 10 to 15 minutes.

In a large bowl, combine the croutons, watermelon cubes, heirloom tomatoes, cherry tomatoes, onion, basil, and pickled watermelon rind. Drizzle with the lemon juice and the remaining 2 tablespoons olive oil. Season generously with salt and toss together. Taste and add more salt if necessary. Let the salad sit for 30 minutes before serving.

Place 1 slice of bacon on each plate. Distribute the salad on top of the bacon and serve.

# FLUKE CEVICHE WITH PINEAPPLE AND CHILIES

Fluke is a wild fish local to the Northeast region. It is mild, with a wonderfully tender texture that absorbs flavors easily. Its sweetness pairs well with fruit; here we chose to use a non-Italian ingredient, pineapple, in a very simple Italian preparation. If fluke is not available, you can use black bass, striped bass, turbot, or hamachi. Although the fish is served raw, we call this ceviche since it is served with an acidic pineapple dressing. Calabrian chilies give the dish a spicy kick that makes each bite memorable.

*Pair with*
AN OFF-DRY RIESLING

The chilled wine cools down the chilies and the sweet Riesling grape complements the pineapple. We like: Hermann J. Wiemer.

## SERVES 4 TO 6

½ of a fresh pineapple

½ teaspoon pureed Calabrian hot chili peppers (see Note), or 1 teaspoon minced red jalapeño pepper

Kosher salt

3 tablespoons freshly squeezed lime juice

1 tablespoon extra-virgin olive oil

8 ounces sushi-grade raw fluke, thinly sliced against the grain

6 fresh mint leaves, thinly sliced or torn into small pieces

Peel the pineapple half and cut it in half again lengthwise. Remove the core from each piece. Finely dice ½ cup of the pineapple and set aside in a small bowl. Coarsely chop the remaining pineapple and puree in a blender. Strain the mixture through a fine-mesh strainer and reserve the juice; discard the solids.

Add the hot chili puree to the diced pineapple and stir together. Stir in 2 tablespoons of the pineapple juice and a pinch of salt. Set aside.

In a small bowl, mix together ¼ cup of the pineapple juice, the lime juice, and olive oil. Season the dressing with a pinch or two of salt.

Place the fluke in a medium bowl and season with salt. Add the pineapple dressing and toss gently to combine.

Using a slotted spoon, remove the fluke from the bowl and arrange on a platter. Scatter the diced pineapple–chili mixture over the fish. Drizzle the entire dish with the pineapple dressing remaining in the bowl. Garnish with the mint and serve immediately.

**NOTE:** Calabrian chilies can be found at Italian specialty stores or easily ordered over the Internet. This recipe calls for the pureed version, but if you can't find the puree, process a few chilies with oil in a mini food processor, or mince them by hand. These chilies are crazy spicy—be careful, a little goes a long way!

# GRILLED SHRIMP WITH ROMESCO SAUCE

I know that *romesco* sauce is Spanish, but it is one of my favorite condiments. At our restaurants, we serve *romesco* sauce with all kinds of dishes, including scallops, quail, and octopus. It is an especially good match for shrimp.

*Pair with*
DRY, AGED
ROSADO

A savory Spanish dish needs a savory Spanish wine: an extremely dry rosé. We like: López de Heredia, the most traditional producer in Rioja.

**SERVES 6**

1 pound (16/20 count) shrimp (3 shrimp per person), shelled and deveined

¼ cup extra-virgin olive oil

Kosher salt and freshly cracked black pepper

1 cup celery leaves

1 cup thinly sliced celery

1 cup thinly sliced cucumber (any kind)

¼ cup fresh flat-leaf parsley leaves

¼ cup thinly sliced red onion

6 to 8 fresh basil leaves, torn

6 to 8 fresh mint leaves, torn

3 tablespoons freshly squeezed lemon juice

Romesco Sauce (recipe follows)

Preheat a grill, grill pan, or broiler to high. In a large bowl, toss the shrimp with 2 tablespoons of the olive oil. Season generously with salt and pepper. Set aside at room temperature until ready to cook.

In a medium bowl, combine the celery leaves, sliced celery, cucumber, parsley, red onion, basil, and mint.

Grill or broil the shrimp for 2 to 3 minutes per side, until cooked through and opaque. Remove from the heat and drizzle with 1 tablespoon of the lemon juice.

Toss the salad ingredients together with the remaining 2 tablespoons olive oil and 2 tablespoons lemon juice. Season with salt to taste.

Place 2 to 3 tablespoons of the Romesco Sauce on each serving plate. Arrange the shrimp decoratively on the sauce. Garnish with the salad.

# ROMESCO SAUCE

This is also delicious as a bruschetta topping or spread on a roasted chicken sandwich.

## MAKES A LITTLE LESS THAN 2 CUPS

2 cups diced red
bell peppers (about
8 ounces; large dice)

½ cup diced
Spanish onion (about
5 ounces; large dice)

16 garlic cloves, halved

1½ teaspoons fresh
thyme leaves

¼ teaspoon red
chili flakes

¼ cup extra-
virgin olive oil

¾ teaspoon kosher salt

½ cup (2½ ounces)
toasted whole
almonds

2½ tablespoons grated
Parmesan cheese

1¾ teaspoons red
wine vinegar

1½ teaspoons water

½ teaspoon pureed
Calabrian chilies
or minced hot
pickled peppers

Preheat the oven to 400°F. Line a baking sheet with parchment paper. In a large bowl, toss together the peppers, onion, garlic, thyme, and chili flakes with 2 tablespoons of the olive oil and ½ teaspoon of the salt. Spread the pepper mixture onto the prepared baking sheet and roast in the oven, stirring occasionally, until the vegetables are slightly golden around the edges and have softened, 35 to 45 minutes. Remove from the oven.

Place the almonds in a food processor and pulse until finely ground. Add the roasted pepper-onion mixture to the food processor along with the Parmesan, vinegar, water, chilies, and the remaining 2 tablespoons olive oil and ¼ teaspoon salt. Blend until smooth. Taste and adjust the seasoning as needed. The sauce can be stored in the refrigerator for 2 to 3 days; bring it to room temperature before serving.

ANTIPASTI

# TUSCAN KALE WITH ROASTED-PEAR VINAIGRETTE

My chef de cuisine at dell'anima, Andrew Whitney, created this dish. Andrew's creativity shines when it comes to food—it would never occur to me to roast a pear and turn it into a creamy vinaigrette. The vinaigrette may look like a mayonnaise-based dressing, but it's nothing like that; it is light and refreshing.

*Pair with*
A GOOD
SOAVE
CLASSICO

The flavors of stone fruit and bitter almonds complement the bitterness of the kale and the pear vinaigrette. We like: Pra.

**SERVES 4 TO 6**

1 large fennel bulb (about 10 ounces)

2 tablespoons extra-virgin olive oil

½ teaspoon kosher salt, plus more for seasoning

1 bunch Tuscan kale (about 7 ounces)

1 Fuji apple, core removed, thinly sliced

½ cup walnuts, broken into small pieces

¼ cup Roasted-Pear Vinaigrette (recipe follows)

Freshly cracked black pepper

1 ounce Pecorino Romano cheese

Preheat the broiler to high. Wash the fennel bulb and cut it in half lengthwise; remove the core. Slice each fennel half lengthwise into ¼-inch-thick pieces. In a medium bowl, toss together the fennel, olive oil, and the ½ teaspoon salt. Spread the fennel out onto a baking sheet. Broil the fennel until all of the pieces are lightly charred, 12 to 15 minutes. Be sure to rotate the pan and toss the fennel frequently so that it cooks evenly.

Remove the stems of the kale leaves. Thinly slice the kale crosswise ("chiffonade"). Place the kale in a large bowl. Add the charred fennel, apple, walnuts, and pear vinaigrette. Season the salad generously with salt and freshly cracked pepper. Toss together. Taste and adjust the seasoning if needed. Feel free to add a little more dressing if the salad seems too dry. Arrange on plates or in serving bowls and garnish with freshly grated Pecorino Romano.

# ROASTED-PEAR VINAIGRETTE

Don't try to use an unripe pear—it's best to wait until pears are super ripe in the fall. This is a great dressing with any fall salad that features a hearty lettuce (radicchio, escarole, or romaine) and fall fruit like pears or apples.

## MAKES 1 CUP

1 large ripe
  Bartlett pear

3 tablespoons extra-
  virgin olive oil

¼ teaspoon kosher
  salt, plus a pinch

1 teaspoon honey

½ teaspoon Dijon
  mustard

2 tablespoons apple
  cider vinegar

2 tablespoons
  apple juice

2 to 4 tablespoons
  water, if necessary

Preheat the broiler to high. Cut the pear lengthwise into 4 quarters. Remove the stem and core. In a small bowl, toss the pear quarters with 1 tablespoon of the olive oil and season with the ¼ teaspoon salt. Place the pear quarters on a baking sheet. Broil the pear, turning frequently, until golden brown on all sides, 5 to 10 minutes.

Roughly chop the roasted pear and place in a blender. Add the honey, mustard, vinegar, apple juice, the remaining 2 tablespoons olive oil, and a pinch of salt. Blend until the dressing has the consistency of a thick, creamy Caesar dressing. If it is too thick, add some water to thin it out. The vinaigrette will keep, refrigerated, for 2 to 3 days.

# ROASTED MUSHROOMS WITH BACON AND EGGS

Some people ask me if crack is an ingredient in this dish—the combination of roasted mushrooms, bacon, and pickled peppers is that good. At L'Artusi, we use a combination of mushrooms, including shiitake, oyster, hon-shimeji, and Trumpet Royale. Feel free to combine any of these. The key is to cook the mushrooms as you would a steak: giving them a caramelized crunchy crust. Be sure to cook them in batches, and do not overcrowd the pan, or the mushrooms will steam instead. This is a great dish for guests because you can cook the mushrooms ahead of time and sauté the rest of the ingredients at the last minute. And don't forget the lemon juice: It ties the whole thing together.

*Pair with*
FULL-FLAVORED, MEDIUM-BODIED BEER

Eggs and beer is one of our favorite pairings. We like: Brooklyn Lager (support your local brewery!).

**SERVES 4**

5 tablespoons extra-virgin olive oil

3 tablespoons unsalted butter

1 pound shiitake mushrooms, stems removed, sliced or torn into ¾-inch-thick pieces (about 6 cups)

¾ teaspoon kosher salt, plus more for seasoning

Freshly cracked black pepper

3½ ounces bacon or pancetta, diced

4 garlic cloves, thinly sliced

2 tablespoons thinly sliced hot pickled peppers (preferably B&G brand, stems and seeds removed; see Note)

6 to 8 fresh basil leaves, torn

Freshly squeezed juice of 1 lemon

4 large eggs (preferably free range, farm fresh)

4 ounces ricotta salata or Parmesan cheese, for garnish

Preheat the oven to 300°F. Heat a large sauté pan over medium-high heat. When hot, add 1 tablespoon of the olive oil and ½ tablespoon of the unsalted butter. Once the butter has melted, add one-third of the mushrooms. Scatter the mushrooms in an even layer in the sauté pan. Cook the mushrooms until caramelized on all sides, 3 to 4 minutes. Season with ¼ teaspoon of the salt and some pepper. Remove the mushrooms from the sauté pan and drain on paper towels. Repeat this process 2 more times with the remaining mushrooms.

# ROASTED MUSHROOMS WITH BACON AND EGGS
**CONTINUED**

Lower the heat to medium, and add 1 tablespoon of the olive oil and 1 tablespoon of the butter to the sauté pan. Add the bacon or pancetta and cook until the fat has rendered and the meat is slightly crispy, 5 to 6 minutes. Add the garlic and cook until the garlic is slightly golden, 1 to 2 minutes longer. Add the pickled peppers and basil; stir to combine. Then add the cooked mushrooms and toss together until the mushrooms are warm. Stir in the lemon juice. Taste and adjust the seasoning as needed; the mixture should be spicy, salty, and lemony. Set aside and keep warm while cooking the eggs.

In a medium ovenproof nonstick sauté pan, heat the remaining 1 tablespoon olive oil and ½ tablespoon butter over medium heat. When the butter has melted, crack the eggs and add them to the pan. Season the eggs generously with salt and pepper. When the eggs start to sizzle, place the sauté pan in the oven. Cook the eggs just until the whites are set but the yolks are still runny, 2 to 3 minutes.

Divide the mushrooms among the serving plates. With a rubber spatula, divide the eggs into individual servings and slide 1 egg onto each serving of mushrooms. Garnish with freshly grated ricotta salata or Parmesan and serve.

**NOTE:** I grew up in Texas, and spicy or acidic foods appeal to me. So I have a hard time not adding hot pickled peppers to everything I make. My preferred brand is B&G, but any hot pickled pepper will do.

# SUMMER SQUASH SALAD WITH CHERRY TOMATOES AND PUMPKIN SEED PESTO VINAIGRETTE

This dish was inspired by a trip to the farmers' market in Union Square. I walked past a farm stand with a plentiful variety of summer squash and decided a raw squash salad was the best way to show off their beauty and flavor. Dressed up with other summer ingredients (tomatoes, basil, and cucumbers), this salad tastes like the farmer's market in each bite.

*Pair with*
VERMENTINO

The grape comes from Liguria (as does pesto), and this crisp white has salty, earthy flavors that complement the dish. We like: Punta Crena.

**SERVES 4 TO 6**

**ANTIPASTI**

## PESTO

½ cup raw pumpkin seeds

¼ cup plus 1 tablespoon extra-virgin olive oil

¼ teaspoon plus ⅛ teaspoon kosher salt

1 large garlic clove (preferably with germ removed; see Note)

1 cup fresh basil leaves

¼ cup grated Parmesan cheese

## PICKLED SHALLOTS

2 shallots, peeled, cut in half lengthwise, and sliced into ⅛-inch-thick half-moons

¾ cup red wine vinegar

1½ tablespoons sugar

1½ tablespoons water

¼ teaspoon kosher salt

## SALAD

Freshly squeezed juice of 2 lemons

2 tablespoons extra-virgin olive oil

2 yellow squash (about 12 ounces total), sliced thin lengthwise on a mandoline

2 zucchini (about 12 ounces total), sliced thin lengthwise on a mandoline

1 pint cherry tomatoes, halved

2 small cucumbers (such as Kirby), halved lengthwise and thinly sliced

1 teaspoon kosher salt

Freshly cracked black pepper

4 ounces feta cheese, crumbled

# SUMMER SQUASH SALAD
**CONTINUED**

To make the pesto, toss together the pumpkin seeds, the 1 tablespoon olive oil, and the ¼ teaspoon salt in a small sauté pan. Place over medium-high heat. Stir frequently until the pumpkin seeds are toasted and start to pop, 4 to 6 minutes; they should be aromatic and slightly puffed. Remove the seeds from the pan to cool.

Place half of the toasted pumpkin seeds and the garlic in a food processor; reserve the remaining pumpkin seeds for garnish. Pulse until finely chopped. Add the basil, Parmesan, and the ⅛ teaspoon salt. Turn the processor on and slowly add the ¼ cup olive oil. When the mixture looks like a paste, taste and adjust the seasoning as needed. Spoon it into a small bowl and set aside in the fridge.

For the pickled shallots, place the shallots in a small heatproof bowl. In a small saucepan, bring the vinegar, sugar, water, and salt to a boil. Pour over the shallots. Let sit at room temperature for at least 30 minutes. The pickled shallots can be made ahead and stored, covered, in the refrigerator.

To make the salad, place ¼ cup of the pesto, the lemon juice, and olive oil in a large bowl. Stir to combine. Drain the liquid from the pickled shallots. To the bowl with the pesto dressing, add the drained pickled shallots, the yellow squash, zucchini, cherry tomatoes, and cucumbers. Add the salt and season generously with freshly cracked pepper. Toss the salad, taste, and adjust the seasoning as needed. Divide the salad among serving plates, and garnish with the feta and reserved toasted pumpkin seeds.

**NOTE:** Without the germ, raw garlic will last longer and will taste less pungent and overwhelming. To remove the germ, slice the garlic clove in half lengthwise. Use a paring knife to remove the piece of germ, or garlic sprout, from the center of each half.

# FARRO-AND-HERB SALAD WITH ROASTED BEETS

Farro is an Italian grain that apparently dates back to Roman times. It's nutty, flavorful, and packed with nutrients and fiber—and unlike barley, wheat berries, or brown rice, it cooks in a relatively short amount of time (15 to 20 minutes). Combined with roasted beets, cucumber, and feta, this is a hearty salad that can be made in advance and served at room temperature, like most antipasti in Italy. We originally served this dish at dell'anima with grilled quail and a dollop of Greek yogurt. If you have access to quail, you should try it. Otherwise, it is equally delicious as a vegetarian dish.

*Pair with* NEGRONI (PAGE 2)

The sweetness balances the bit of chili heat in the salad. And this salad is the kind of dish you'd find at a classic *aperitivo* hour, so a classic cocktail is in order.

## SERVES 4 TO 6

### ROASTED BEETS

- 1 pound beets, scrubbed and stems removed
- 2 tablespoons extra-virgin olive oil
- 2 teaspoons kosher salt
- ½ cup water, plus more as needed

### SALAD

- 1 teaspoon kosher salt, plus more for cooking the farro
- 1 cup farro
- 5 tablespoons extra-virgin olive oil
- 1 cup diced cucumber (see Note)
- ½ cup feta or diced ricotta salata cheese
- ¼ cup thinly sliced scallion
- 1 tablespoon finely grated lemon zest
- 1 tablespoon minced hot chili pepper (red or green)
- 2 sprigs fresh flat-leaf parsley, roughly chopped
- 5 leaves fresh basil, torn
- 5 leaves fresh mint, torn
- 1 garlic clove, grated on a Microplane
- ¼ cup freshly squeezed lemon juice

To roast the beets, preheat the oven to 350°F. Place the beets, olive oil, and salt in an ovenproof medium (2- or 3-quart) dish with a lid; toss to coat the beets. Pour the ½ cup water into the dish; add more water as necessary to reach a depth of ¼ inch. Roast until the beets are easily pierced with a metal skewer; depending on the size of the beets, this will take anywhere from 1 to 1½ hours.

Remove from the oven and let cool. When the beets are cool enough to touch, use a paring knife to remove and discard the skins. Dice the beets into ¼-inch cubes.

To make the salad, bring a large pot of water to a boil and add a generous amount of salt. Taste the water to make sure that it is salty. Boil the farro until cooked through, 15 to 20 minutes. Drain thoroughly. Toss the farro with 1 tablespoon of the olive oil.

In a large salad bowl, combine the cooked farro, the cucumber, cheese, scallion, lemon zest, chili pepper, parsley, basil, mint, and garlic. Season with the 1 teaspoon salt and drizzle with the lemon juice and the remaining 4 tablespoons olive oil. Toss the salad; taste and adjust the seasoning if needed. Right before serving, add the diced roasted beets and toss. Serve at room temperature.

**NOTE:** You can use any kind of cucumber you like and peel it or not according to taste (but it's best to peel it if the skin is especially thick or waxy).

# LEMON PICCATA SWEETBREADS WITH CELERY ROOT PUREE

Sweetbreads have found a new audience among the younger foodie crowd and the more sophisticated mature crowd. Even our toddler, Luke, loves them—he thinks they are chicken nuggets. Dusted in semolina flour and pan-fried, these have a crunchy exterior and a tender interior. Do not be intimidated by the length of this recipe. Both the poached sweetbreads and the celery root puree can be prepared a day or two in advance; after that, the rest takes 30 minutes at most.

**SERVES 4 TO 6**

## CELERY ROOT PUREE

2 cups peeled, diced celery root

1⅓ cups water

⅓ cup heavy cream

1 teaspoon kosher salt, plus more for seasoning

½ bay leaf

1 strip of peeled lemon zest (about ½ inch by 1 inch)

2 tablespoons extra-virgin olive oil

## SWEETBREADS

Poached sweetbreads (recipe follows)

Kosher salt and freshly cracked black pepper

6 tablespoons semolina flour (or unbleached all-purpose flour, fine cornmeal, or rice flour)

Oil for frying (olive oil, peanut, or vegetable oil)

## LEMON-CAPER SAUCE

½ cup plus 3 tablespoons unsalted butter

1 tablespoon plus 1 teaspoon capers

2 teaspoons julienned lemon zest

¼ cup water

2 tablespoons freshly squeezed lemon juice

2 teaspoons finely chopped fresh parsley

Kosher salt for seasoning (optional)

To make the celery root puree, place the celery root, water, heavy cream, ¾ teaspoon of the salt, the bay leaf, and strip of lemon zest in a small saucepan. Cover and place over high heat. As soon as the mixture reaches a boil, turn the heat down to low. Cook until the celery root is very tender when pierced with a fork, 10 to 15 minutes. Be sure to stir occasionally to make sure that no pieces are stuck to the bottom of the saucepan.

Remove the saucepan from the heat and drain the celery root, reserving the cooking liquid. Discard the bay leaf and lemon zest. Place the celery root in a blender along with 1 cup of the cooking liquid, the olive oil, and the remaining ¼ teaspoon salt. Blend together until smooth. The puree should have the consistency of baby food. If it appears to be too thick, add a little more cooking liquid. Taste and add another pinch or two of salt, if necessary. Return the puree to the saucepan. Cover and keep in a warm place at the back of the stove until ready to serve. The puree can be made ahead and reheated gently over low heat, adding a little more water to thin it out, if necessary. While it is ideal to serve the puree warm, it is equally delicious at room temperature.

To make the sweetbreads, season the poached sweetbreads generously on all sides with salt and freshly cracked black pepper. Place the semolina flour in a shallow bowl. Toss the sweetbreads in the semolina flour to coat them.

Heat a large sauté pan or cast-iron skillet over high heat. Add enough frying oil to reach a depth of ¼ inch. When the oil is hot, decrease the heat to medium. Gently add the sweetbreads, one at a time, to the pan. Be very careful, as the moisture in the sweetbreads will make the oil splatter. Do not leave them unattended on the stove. Cook the sweetbreads for 2 minutes, or until golden brown on the bottom. Use tongs to turn them over and cook the other side for another 2 minutes. The sweetbreads should be evenly golden brown on all sides. Depending on the heat of the oil, the total cooking time should be 4 to 5 minutes. Remove the sweetbreads from the hot pan and place on a plate lined with paper towels to remove any excess fat.

To make the lemon-caper sauce, place the 3 tablespoons butter, the capers, and the julienned lemon zest in a medium sauté pan over high heat. Cook the butter-lemon mixture, swirling the pan regularly, until the butter is evenly browned and very aromatic. Remove the pan from the heat and slowly add ¼ cup water to stop the butter from cooking and turning too dark. Swirl the pan to incorporate the water into the brown butter.

Return the pan to the stove over very low heat. Add the lemon juice and stir to combine. Slowly whisk in the ½ cup butter, 1 tablespoon at a time. Be sure to whisk each piece of butter into the sauce. When the butter is almost melted into the sauce, add the next piece of butter. Continue this process until all of the butter is emulsified in the sauce. Stir in the parsley. Taste the sauce and add a couple of pinches of salt, if necessary.

On warmed plates, place a large spoonful (approximately 2 tablespoons) of celery root puree on each plate. Spread the puree out so that it coats the plate. Divide the sweetbreads among the plates, on top of the puree. Spoon a generous amount of sauce on top of and around the sweetbreads. Serve immediately.

# LEMON PICCATA SWEETBREADS WITH CELERY ROOT PUREE
**CONTINUED**

## POACHED SWEETBREADS

Be sure to plan ahead and ask your local butcher for sweetbreads. Depending on availability, it may take a few days to order. Or you can order them online from dartagnan.com.

**MAKES ENOUGH FOR 4 TO 6 SERVINGS**

1 lobe of sweetbreads (about 1 pound)

7 cups water

1 medium carrot, peeled and sliced into 1-inch-thick pieces

1 celery stalk, cut into 1-inch-thick pieces

½ Spanish onion, cut into 4 pieces

1 bay leaf

1 teaspoon black peppercorns

1 tablespoon kosher salt

1 lemon

Place the sweetbreads, water, carrot, celery, onion, bay leaf, peppercorns, and salt in a medium (3-quart) saucepan. Cut the lemon in half and remove the seeds. Squeeze the lemon juice into the pan and place the lemon halves in the water.

Bring the mixture to a boil over high heat. Immediately turn the heat down to low. The water should be at just under a simmer. Poach the sweetbreads until easily pierced with a metal skewer, approximately 30 minutes. The cooked sweetbreads will have the color of a cooked chicken breast.

Remove the sweetbreads from the hot poaching liquid. Let cool to room temperature and then refrigerate them overnight, or until cold.

To clean the sweetbreads, use a paring knife to discard any darkened or discolored dark purple areas. Gently peel off the membrane on the exterior of the sweetbreads; it will look and feel similar to the skin on a hard-boiled egg.

Using your hands, gently tear apart the sweetbreads into nugget-sized pieces, about 1 inch by ½ inch. The sweetbreads have a natural way of splitting apart. If some pieces seem too large, use a knife to cut into smaller nuggets. Ideally all of the sweetbread pieces will be about the same size. This will help ensure even cooking. The sweetbreads can be stored in an airtight container in the refrigerator for 2 to 3 days before serving, but are best eaten as soon as possible.

# ROASTED ACORN SQUASH WITH RADICCHIO

Radicchio is extremely bitter and can be overpowering, but it is one of my favorite ingredients. In this salad, the radicchio complements the sweetness of the roasted squash and the sweet-and-sour raisins. The aged cheese adds richness to each bite.

*Pair with*
A MALTY
BROWN ALE

The ale should combine bitter and sweet, with nutty notes to complement the nutty flavor of the squash. We like: Captain Lawrence Brown Bird Ale.

## SERVES 4 TO 6

ANTIPASTI

### ROASTED SQUASH AND ONIONS

| | | |
|---|---|---|
| 2 acorn squash (about 1½ pounds) | 2 teaspoons unsalted butter | 2 tablespoons maple syrup |
| 6 tablespoons extra-virgin olive oil | 8 sage leaves, torn into ½-inch pieces | 12 cipollini onions, halved |
| Kosher salt | | |

### SALAD

| | | |
|---|---|---|
| 3 tablespoons golden raisins | ½ cup pecans, broken into small pieces | 3 to 4 tablespoons extra-virgin olive oil |
| ¼ cup red wine vinegar | Kosher salt and freshly cracked black pepper | 1 ounce Fiore Sardo (see Note) or aged Pecorino cheese |
| 1 head of radicchio (about 7 ounces) | | |

To make the squash and onions, preheat the oven to 350°F. Cut each squash in half. Remove and discard the seeds. Cut each half into 4 wedges, each wedge about 1 inch thick. In a large bowl, toss the squash wedges together with 2 tablespoons of the olive oil and season generously with salt.

Heat a large sauté pan over medium-high heat. Add 1 tablespoon of the olive oil and 1 teaspoon of the butter. As soon as the butter melts, add half of the squash to the pan, arranging the pieces so that they are cut side down. Sprinkle half of the sage over the squash. Cook undisturbed until the squash is golden brown on 1 side, 2 to 3 minutes. Turn each squash piece over and cook for another 2 to 3 minutes, until golden brown on the other side. Remove the squash from the pan and place on a baking sheet.

Repeat this process with 1 tablespoon of the olive oil, the remaining 1 teaspoon butter, and the remaining squash and sage leaves. You may need 2 baking sheets. Drizzle the maple syrup over the squash segments on the baking sheet(s).

# ROASTED ACORN SQUASH WITH RADICCHIO
**CONTINUED**

In a small bowl, toss the onions with the remaining 2 tablespoons olive oil. Season generously with salt. Scatter the onions among the squash pieces on the baking sheet(s). Place the baking sheet(s) in the oven and bake until each piece of squash is easily pierced with a fork and the onions are lightly golden and tender, 25 to 30 minutes. Set aside.

To make the salad, place the raisins in a small bowl. In a small saucepan, bring the red wine vinegar to a boil. Pour over the raisins and set aside for 15 minutes.

Meanwhile, discard the outside layers of the radicchio. Cut the head of radicchio in half lengthwise and remove the core. Gently remove the radicchio leaves and roughly tear each leaf into 1-inch pieces.

Place the radicchio in a large salad bowl with the roasted squash, roasted onions, and pecans. Drain the raisins, saving the vinegar. Add the raisins to the radicchio mixture. Season the salad with kosher salt and freshly cracked black pepper. Drizzle 2 tablespoons of the reserved red wine vinegar over the salad along with 3 tablespoons of olive oil. Toss together. If the salad seems too dry, add a little more vinegar and olive oil. Taste and adjust the seasoning if needed.

Arrange the squash pieces on serving plates. Distribute the rest of the salad on top of the squash pieces. Garnish with freshly grated Fiore Sardo.

**NOTE:** *Fiore Sardo* is an aged sheep's milk cheese from Sardinia. If it's unavailable, feel free to substitute another aged sheep's milk cheese or Pecorino Romano.

# ROASTED ASPARAGUS WITH YOGURT AND POACHED EGGS

This dish was created about 30 minutes before we first served it at L'Artusi. We had a ton of fresh, beautiful asparagus on hand and I looked around the kitchen to see what ingredients we could pair it with. The answer was yogurt and eggs—and this dish sold more than any other that night. Feel free to grill the asparagus, if you want, and/or to fry the eggs instead of poaching them, if preferred. As you might imagine, this dish is perfect for breakfast, too.

*Pair with*
SAUVIGNON
BLANC

This is one of the few wines that go well with asparagus. We like: Ronco delle Mele from Venica & Venica; its grapefruit-citrus flavors complement the Greek yogurt.

## SERVES 4

½ cup Greek yogurt, preferably whole fat

¼ cup plus 2 tablespoons extra-virgin olive oil

2 teaspoons kosher salt, plus more for seasoning

Freshly cracked black pepper

1 bunch of asparagus

2 tablespoons white vinegar

4 large eggs

2 ounces Parmesan or ricotta salata cheese

In a small bowl, stir together the yogurt, the 2 tablespoons olive oil, ½ teaspoon of the salt, and 4 turns of cracked black pepper. Chill the yogurt sauce until ready to serve.

Preheat the broiler to high. Cut off the tough bottoms of the asparagus spears. Spread out the asparagus on a baking sheet; drizzle with the ¼ cup olive oil and season with the remaining 1½ teaspoons salt and a generous amount of pepper. Shake the pan to coat the asparagus. Broil until slightly golden brown and tender, checking the asparagus every couple of minutes and gently shaking the pan to rotate the asparagus, 5 to 8 minutes, depending on the size of the spears. Remove from the oven and let sit at room temperature while poaching the eggs.

In a heavy-duty 3-quart saucepan, bring 1 quart of water to a simmer. Add the white vinegar and season the water with salt. Lower the heat so that the water remains just under a simmer. Slowly crack each egg into the water. Let the eggs fall gently, and make sure to give each egg enough space from the others. If any of the eggs appear to be sticking to the bottom of the pan, use a rubber spatula to gently dislodge them; the eggs should cook suspended in the water. The eggs are finished poaching when the whites are firm and the yolks are slightly runny, about 4 minutes. Test each egg individually by gently removing it from the water with a slotted spoon and pressing your finger against the egg to make sure the yolk is soft. Place the poached eggs on a plate lined with paper towels.

Distribute the yogurt sauce among 4 serving plates. Divide the roasted asparagus among the plates. Using a spoon, gently remove the eggs, one at a time, and place on the asparagus. Sprinkle each egg with a pinch of salt and a couple of turns of pepper. Garnish each plate with freshly grated Parmesan or ricotta salata.

# ROASTED SHIITAKE MUSHROOM AND SPINACH SALAD

My wife deserves all of the credit for this dish. When she was going through her brief vegan phase, this was her go-to salad (without the Parmesan). Although absolutely delicious that way, I can't help but add cheese to all of my salads.

**SERVES 4 TO 6**

*Pair with*
ORANGE
WINE

This white wine made with extended skin contact picks up on the earthy mushroom flavors. We like: Coenobium Rusticum, served at red wine temperature.

1 pound shiitake mushrooms, stems removed, sliced ¼ inch thick (if very large, cut in half and then sliced ¼ inch thick)

½ cup extra-virgin olive oil

1½ teaspoons kosher salt

Freshly cracked black pepper

½ cup whole almonds

6 tablespoons minced shallots

2 teaspoons unsalted butter

¼ cup red wine vinegar

6 ounces fresh baby spinach

⅓ cup grated Parmesan cheese

Preheat the oven to 400°F. In a large bowl, toss together the shiitake mushrooms, ¼ cup of the olive oil, 1 teaspoon of the salt, and about 12 turns of black pepper. Distribute the mushrooms onto a baking sheet. There should be plenty of space around the mushrooms. If the mushrooms appear to be too crowded, use 2 baking sheets. Roast the mushrooms in the oven until golden brown and crispy, 20 to 25 minutes. Remove from the oven.

Decrease the oven temperature to 350°F. Place the almonds on a baking sheet or in an ovenproof sauté pan. Toast in the oven until aromatic, about 7 minutes. Remove from the oven and place the almonds on a cold plate to cool. When cool enough to touch, use a chef's knife to roughly chop the toasted almonds.

To make the dressing, place the shallots, 2 tablespoons of the olive oil, the butter, and the remaining ½ teaspoon salt in a medium sauté pan over medium heat. Cook for 2 to 3 minutes, stirring occasionally, until the shallots have softened and appear translucent. Add the red wine vinegar. Bring to a simmer and turn off the heat.

To assemble the salad, place the spinach, roasted mushrooms, toasted almonds, and warm dressing in a large salad bowl. Drizzle with the remaining 2 tablespoons olive oil. Sprinkle generously with freshly cracked black pepper and half of the grated Parmesan. Toss together the salad ingredients. Taste and adjust the seasoning as needed. Serve the salad immediately with the remaining grated Parmesan on top.

*Chapter 3*

# PRIMI

*Primo* is considered the first warm course of an Italian meal (antipasti usually being cold and more of a snack). At our restaurants, we treat *primi* as mid-courses. The hope is that our guests will share a pasta or polenta and then try out a *secondo* afterward. This is where portion sizes come into play. Almost all of the recipes in this chapter serve 4 to 6: Six mid-course portions—small enough to allow you to enjoy the taste of the dish without filling you up completely—or four main courses.

Most of these recipes are for pasta—my favorite thing to eat and to make. Unfortunately, most of us grew up in homes where pasta was made incorrectly. The pasta water wasn't salty enough. The overcooked pasta was drained and rinsed. Finally, the pasta was served separately from the sauce. Forget all this. Here's how to make pasta the *right* way:

**USE HIGH-QUALITY DRIED PASTA.** If you're not making fresh pasta, look for texture in packaged pasta, so the sauce will cling to the noodle. Dried pasta should have a white crackle, or stubble; avoid shiny pasta. At the restaurants, we use Rustichella d'Abruzzo dried pasta. Other brands I like: Bartolini, Setaro, DeLallo, Garofalo, and Whole Foods 365.

**BOIL IT IN SALTY WATER.** Really salty. Pasta noodles are tasteless. Even if your sauce is well seasoned, the dish will still taste bland if the pasta water isn't salty enough. It should taste like the sea. A good ratio is 4 quarts water to ½ cup kosher salt.

**UNDERCOOK IT SLIGHTLY.** Pasta should be al dente when removed from the water; when you break a noodle, there will be a thin white line inside. The magic happens when you add the pasta to the sauce: The noodles finish cooking and absorb the delicious sauce.

**DON'T DRAIN IT!** Remove pasta from the water with a spider (skimmer), slotted spoon, tongs, or a pasta basket to place it in the sauce. You *want* that excess pasta water that clings to the pasta—it helps season the sauce and gives the sauce a looser consistency.

**SERVE PASTA IN WARM BOWLS.** Before bringing the pasta water to a boil, place your serving bowls in a 200°F oven or put them in the microwave for a minute or two.

**DRIZZLE WITH HIGH-QUALITY EXTRA-VIRGIN OLIVE OIL:** It will add flavor and a silky texture. We recommend Frantoia, Olio Verde, Capezzana, or Laudemio.

**GARNISH WITH FRESHLY GRATED CHEESE:** Have large chunks of Parmesan and pecorino on hand, and invest in a Microplane grater to grate with ease.

*— Gabriel Thompson*

PRIMI

# RISOTTO ALLA PILOTA

*Pilota* was the term for a rice mill worker when the work was still done by hand. They needed a hearty dish to sustain them, so *pilotas* in Verona added ground pork and cheese to their rice. This is not your typical creamy risotto; it's more like Italian fried rice. The rice is boiled like pasta and then simmered in chicken stock until almost dry. The only creaminess comes from the butter and cheese. If you're looking to go off your diet, this dish is the best reason ever.

*Pair with*
A BUBBLY RED
LAMBRUSCO

We like: Lini 910 Lambrusco Rosso—this intensely flavorful wine matches the meaty character of the dish, while the bubbles cut through the richness.

## SERVES 4 TO 6

Kosher salt

8 ounces short-grain rice, such as Arborio or Vialone Nano

2 tablespoons extra-virgin olive oil

1½ cups small dice yellow onions

6 to 8 fresh sage leaves, torn into small pieces

5 to 6 ounces spicy Italian sausage, casings removed

1 cup small dice Italian salumi (such as sopressata, finocchiona, and/ or pepperoni)

2 cups chicken stock

¼ cup freshly grated Pecorino Romano cheese

2 tablespoons unsalted butter, diced

¼ cup finely chopped fresh flat-leaf parsley

2 tablespoons high-quality extra-virgin olive oil

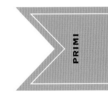

PRIMI

Bring a large pot of water to a boil. Season generously with salt. Boil the rice for 7 minutes (it will not be fully cooked). Drain the rice, spread it out onto a baking sheet, and let it cool while you prepare the rest of the dish.

Heat the olive oil, onions, and sage in a large sauté pan over medium-high heat. Season with salt. Cook, stirring occasionally, until the onions start to caramelize, about 5 minutes.

Add the Italian sausage. Break the sausage into small pieces. When the meat starts to caramelize (about 3 minutes), add the salumi and sauté for another 3 minutes. Add the rice and let the rice toast for a minute or two.

Add the chicken stock and simmer until almost all of the moisture has evaporated, 7 to 8 minutes. Taste the rice. If it is not thoroughly cooked, add a little more chicken stock. The rice is ready when it is cooked through and there is very little moisture in the pan (unlike a creamy risotto). The mixture should look like fried rice.

Add the cheese, butter, parsley, and high-quality olive oil. Serve immediately.

# GARGANELLI WITH MUSHROOM RAGÙ

Vegetarians swear that there is meat in this sauce. That's because the mushrooms, cooked to near-oblivion, eventually take on a deep, rich flavor that can rival that of any Bolognese. Even kids will love it. Our son, Luke, cannot get enough of this pasta.

**SERVES 4 TO 6**

*Pair with*
A DRY, EARTHY
RED WINE

Nebbiolo and mushrooms are made for each other. We like: Albino Rocca Nebbiolo d'Alba.

8 ounces fresh cremini mushrooms

1½ tablespoons extra-virgin olive oil

1 cup small dice Spanish onion

½ teaspoon kosher salt, plus more for cooking the pasta

½ tablespoon tomato paste

½ tablespoon porcini powder (or ground dried porcini mushrooms)

¼ cup dry white wine, such as Pinot Grigio

¼ cup heavy cream

14 ounces fresh or frozen garganelli (see page 107) or dried penne

¼ cup freshly grated Parmesan cheese, plus more as needed

1 tablespoon plus 1 teaspoon unsalted butter, cut into small pieces

4 ounces ricotta salata

To prep the mushrooms, remove a sliver off the bottoms of the mushroom stems and discard. Coarsely chop the mushrooms by hand into ½-inch pieces. Place the mushrooms in a food processor. Turn the machine on for a few seconds. Scrape the sides of the bowl with a spatula. Turn the machine on again. Continue this process until the mushrooms are finely chopped.

In a large sauté pan, combine the olive oil, onion, and the ½ teaspoon salt. Place over medium-high heat. Cook, stirring frequently, until the onion is soft and starts to take on a little color, 5 to 6 minutes.

Decrease the heat to medium and add the tomato paste. Cook, stirring constantly, until the tomato paste starts to brown, about 2 minutes.

Add the finely chopped mushrooms and the mushroom powder. Stirring frequently, cook the mushrooms until there is no moisture and the mushrooms have caramelized and are dark brown. As you scrape the bottom of the pan, the mixture will eventually clump together into a very unattractive mixture. The mushrooms will take 15 to 20 minutes to cook properly.

Add the white wine and cook, stirring constantly, until the mixture is completely dry. Add the heavy cream and cook until the mixture barely has any moisture. The sauce is ready for the pasta at this point.

Meanwhile, in a large pot of salted boiling water, cook the garganelli until al dente. If the pasta is freshly made, it will take 2 to 3 minutes. If it is frozen, it may take a minute or two longer. The pasta will float to the top when it is ready. (If using dried penne, cook until al dente, slightly less than the suggested cooking time on the package.) Reserve the pasta water.

Add the pasta to the mushroom sauce. Over medium-low heat, add the ¼ cup Parmesan, the butter, and ½ cup of the pasta water. Toss together. Simmer for a minute or two and gently coat the pasta in the mushroom sauce, thinning the sauce with pasta water or simmering 1 to 2 minutes more and adding a little more Parmesan to thicken as needed.  Serve with freshly grated ricotta salata.

PRIMI

# FARFALLE WITH DUCK RAGÙ

Katherine introduced me to this dish. While she was working at Italian Wine Merchants, the owner, Sergio Esposito, taught Katherine how to make a similar braise using rabbit. The beauty of this braise is that it is easy to make and spectacular with almost any protein. I have made variations with chicken legs, pork shoulder, and lamb shank. But my favorite is duck legs.

*Pair with*
CALIFORNIA
PINOT NOIR

Choose one from a coastal cool climate, with a lightness to contrast with duck's deep flavor. We like: Sandhi Pinot Noir.

**SERVES 4 TO 6**

2 duck legs (about 1 pound)

1 teaspoon kosher salt, plus more for seasoning

Freshly cracked black pepper

5 tablespoons extra-virgin olive oil

1¼ cups small dice yellow onions

½ cup diced shallots

¼ cup chopped garlic

¼ teaspoon red chili flakes, plus more to taste

1 cup dry white wine, such as Pinot Grigio

1 cup chicken stock

1 cup diced canned tomatoes, with juice

2 sprigs fresh thyme

1 sprig fresh rosemary

1 bay leaf

10 ounces farfalle, fresh (see page 107) or dried

3½ tablespoons grated Pecorino Romano cheese, plus more for garnish

2 tablespoons chopped fresh flat-leaf parsley

Preheat the oven to 300°F. Season the duck legs generously with salt and pepper. Place a large sauté pan or cast-iron skillet over high heat. Add 1 tablespoon of the olive oil to the hot pan. Gently add the duck legs to the pan, skin side down. Cook undisturbed until the duck skin is golden and releases easily from the pan, 4 to 5 minutes. Turn the duck over to sear the other side, 2 to 3 minutes more. Remove the duck from the pan and set aside on a plate while preparing the braising mixture.

Heat 2 tablespoons of the olive oil in a medium (3-quart) ovenproof saucepan or Dutch oven over high heat. Add the onions, shallots, garlic, the ¼ teaspoon chili flakes, and the 1 teaspoon salt. Sauté the mixture, stirring frequently, until the onions are soft and start to take on a little golden color, about 6 minutes. Add the white wine and cook until no liquid remains, about 5 minutes. Add the chicken stock, canned tomatoes, thyme, rosemary, and bay leaf. Bring the mixture to a boil, then decrease the heat to low. Add the duck legs to the pan. Cover and place in the oven to braise until tender, 1½ to 2 hours. They are ready when easily pierced with a metal skewer or a fork; the meat should easily release from the bone, and easily tear apart with a fork and tongs. If there is any tension, continue braising for another 15 to 20 minutes and check again.

Once the duck legs are ready, remove them from the braising mixture and set aside on a plate or cutting board to cool (see Note). Return the pan to the stovetop and simmer over medium heat until most of the liquid has evaporated and the sauce is thick, about 20 minutes. Remove the thyme, rosemary, and bay leaf. Taste the sauce and add a pinch or two of salt if necessary (keeping in mind that salty Pecorino will be added to the pasta).

Remove the duck meat from the bones and roughly chop. Add the chopped duck meat back to the sauce. The duck ragù can be made in advance and stored in an airtight container in the refrigerator for 3 to 4 days or in the freezer for 2 weeks. Bring to a simmer over medium-high heat in a large sauté pan before continuing.

To make the pasta, bring a large pot of water to a boil. Season generously with salt. Keep the duck ragù over low heat while cooking the pasta.

Boil the pasta until just al dente. If using fresh pasta, the pasta will cook relatively quickly (about 2 minutes). If using dried pasta, cook the pasta until al dente, slightly less than the suggested cooking time on the package. Cut 1 bow tie open to make sure there is a thin white line in the center. The pasta will finish cooking in the sauce. Reserve the pasta water.

Add the pasta to the duck ragù. Stir to combine. Add the 3½ tablespoons Pecorino, the parsley, and the remaining 2 tablespoons olive oil. If desired, add a pinch of red chili flakes to heighten the spice. Toss together, thinning the sauce with pasta water or simmering for 1 to 2 minutes more to thicken as needed. Serve immediately in warm bowls. Garnish with additional Pecorino, if desired.

**NOTE:** As in Gnocchi with Braised Chicken (page 83), I like to roast the duck skin, finely chop it, and stir it back into the ragù, giving the sauce a rich depth of flavor. To do this, peel the skin off of the braised duck legs. Lay the skins flat on a baking sheet lined with parchment or a Silpat. Roast the duck skin in a 350°F oven for 20 to 30 minutes, until the skin is a deep golden brown color. Once the skin is cool enough to handle, finely chop and add to the duck ragù.

# LAMB BOLOGNESE WITH SPINACH TAGLIATELLE

Traditional bolognese is made with a combination of pork, veal, and beef. Our untraditional version uses ground lamb instead. If you feel like experimenting, you can include additional vegetables; or use red wine instead of white. In almost any variation, the result will be delicious. Any bolognese left over is excellent served on crusty rolls like an Italian Sloppy Joe. This is how we serve the lamb bolognese at Anfora.

*Pair with*
A SAVORY, EARTHY RED WINE

To complement this dish you want a wine that's dark and meaty but not overbearing. We like: Copain Syrah.

**SERVES 4 TO 6**

- 12 to 14 ounces ground lamb
- 1 teaspoon plus ½ teaspoon kosher salt, plus more for seasoning
- Freshly cracked black pepper
- 2 tablespoons extra-virgin olive oil
- 1 cup small dice yellow onion

- 3 minced garlic cloves
- 1 sprig fresh thyme
- 1 bay leaf
- ¼ teaspoon red chili flakes
- 1 tablespoon tomato paste
- ½ cup dry white wine, such as Pinot Grigio

- 1 cup pureed fresh or canned crushed tomatoes, with juice
- ½ cup chicken stock
- 15 ounces spinach tagliatelle (page 108)
- ¼ cup grated Pecorino Romano cheese, plus more for garnish
- 3 tablespoons high-quality extra-virgin olive oil

In a large bowl, season the ground lamb with the 1 teaspoon salt and several turns of black pepper. Mix to evenly distribute the salt and pepper.

Line a plate with paper towels. Place a large sauté pan over high heat. Add the olive oil. When the oil is hot, add half of the ground meat. Use a wooden spoon to break up the meat into smaller pieces. Cook until the meat is browned on all sides, about 4 minutes. Transfer the meat from the pan to the prepared plate. Repeat this process with the remaining meat. Set aside the browned meat.

Add the onion, garlic, thyme, bay leaf, chili flakes, and the ½ teaspoon salt to the pan. Cook the onion mixture, stirring frequently, until the onion is soft and starts to take on a slight golden color, about 5 minutes.

Add the tomato paste. Constantly stirring and scraping the bottom of the pan, cook until the tomato paste is slightly browned, about 2 minutes. Add the lamb and stir to combine.

Add the white wine and cook until the wine evaporates completely, 3 to 4 minutes. Add the pureed tomatoes and chicken stock. Bring to a boil, then decrease the heat to low and simmer for 30 minutes. Taste and adjust the seasoning, if necessary. The bolognese can be made ahead to this point and stored in an airtight container in the refrigerator for 3 to 4 days or in the freezer for 2 weeks; bring to a simmer, then keep over low heat before continuing.

To cook the pasta, bring a large pot of water to a boil. Season the water generously with salt. Boil the spinach tagliatelle until al dente, about 2 minutes. Taste the pasta periodically to check if it is cooked, but still chewy in the center. Transfer the cooked pasta to the sauce and gently stir to coat the noodles with the sauce. Reserve the pasta water.

Add the ¼ cup grated Pecorino and the high-quality olive oil. Stir together, thinning the sauce with pasta water or simmering 1 to 2 minutes more to thicken as needed. Serve immediately in warm bowls, garnished with extra grated Pecorino, if desired.

# ORECCHIETTE WITH PEAS AND BACON

Orecchiette's small round indented shape gives it its playful name, which means "little ears." The dented side is perfect for catching small chunks in pasta sauce like peas or diced bacon. In the spring, we serve this dish with freshly shucked peas from the farmer's market. At home, I make it all year round with frozen peas.

*Pair with*
DARK-COLORED, LIGHT-BODIED BEER

We like: Greenport Black Duck Porter—the roasted malt gives it a nice smokiness to go with the bacon. Plus it's local!

## SERVES 4

PRIMI

4 tablespoons unsalted butter

4 ounces bacon, small dice

1 cup small dice Spanish onion

¾ teaspoon kosher salt, plus more for seasoning

½ cup dry white wine, such as Pinot Grigio

½ cup chicken or vegetable stock or Parmesan Brodo (recipe follows)

10 ounces dried orecchiette

1 cup frozen peas (see Note)

¼ cup freshly grated Parmesan cheese, plus more as needed

3 tablespoons chopped fresh flat-leaf parsley

Freshly cracked black pepper

1 tablespoon high-quality extra-virgin olive oil

In a large sauté pan, melt 2 tablespoons of the butter over medium-high heat. Once the butter is melted and begins to turn golden brown, 1 to 2 minutes, add the bacon. Sauté the bacon until the fat has rendered and the bacon is slightly crispy, about 2 minutes. Add the onion and the ¾ teaspoon salt. Sauté until the onion is softened and begins to take on a golden color, 3 to 5 minutes.

Add the wine and cook until there is no moisture left in the pan, about 3 minutes. Add the stock and decrease the heat to low. Taste and adjust the seasoning as needed. Keep the bacon-onion mixture warm over low heat.

Meanwhile, bring a large pot of water to a boil. Season generously with salt. Place the orecchiette in the boiling water. Cook the orecchiette until just al dente, slightly less than the suggested cooking time on the package. There should be a thin white line running through the center of the pasta. Reserve the pasta water.

Meanwhile, a minute before the pasta is ready, add the peas to the bacon-onion mixture.

## ORECCHIETTE WITH PEAS AND BACON
**CONTINUED**

When the pasta is al dente, use a spider or slotted spoon to add it to the bacon, onion, and peas. Toss together and increase the heat to medium-low. Add the ¼ cup Parmesan, the remaining 2 tablespoons butter, the parsley, a generous amount of freshly cracked black pepper, and the high-quality olive oil. Toss together and simmer for 1 to 2 minutes, thinning the sauce with pasta water or simmering 1 to 2 minutes more and adding a little more Parmesan to thicken as needed. Serve immediately in warm bowls.

**NOTE:** If using fresh peas, blanch them in boiling salted water for 2 minutes before adding to the bacon-onion mixture.

## PARMESAN BRODO

This is a kind of Parmesan tea: Parmesan rinds are slowly cooked in hot water, disintegrating over time and creating an unbelievably delicious and rich Parmesan stock. This *brodo*, or broth, is excellent in soups and pasta sauces. In fact, my favorite impromptu pasta sauce is a combination of sautéed garlic, Parmesan *brodo*, butter, and grated Parmesan, slowly stirred together on low heat. Perfect with spaghetti.

### MAKES JUST UNDER 2 QUARTS

4 ounces Parmesan cheese rinds, large or small pieces

2 quarts water

Place the Parmesan rinds and the water in a medium (3-quart) saucepan. Bring to a simmer, stirring frequently. Decrease the heat to low. Cook the Parmesan *brodo* for 1 hour and 15 minutes, stirring and scraping the bottom of the pan every 5 to 10 minutes. It is important to keep the rind and cheese from sticking to the bottom of the pan (see Note). Do not let the mixture simmer while the *brodo* is cooking. The liquid should be hot, but just under a simmer. Turn off the heat and let the *brodo* sit at room temperature for 30 to 45 minutes.

Pour the *brodo* into a container, leaving the rinds and any melted cheese behind in the pan. (The rinds will naturally sink to the bottom of the pan and are unlikely to pour into the container.) Once the *brodo* is cool, store it covered in the refrigerator for 4 to 5 days, or in the freezer for several weeks. If you're freezing it, feel free to store the *brodo* in more manageable portion sizes, such as in an ice cube tray or in 1-cup containers.

**NOTE:** A few suggestions when making the Parmesan *brodo:* Frequently scrape the rinds from the bottom of the pan when cooking; if ignored, the cheese will burn. Do not use a strainer; the strainer will become impossible to clean. Do not try this with pecorino rinds. I did. It was disgusting.

# GNOCCHI WITH BRAISED CHICKEN

This is chicken and dumplings on steroids. Chicken legs are slowly braised in a white wine–vegetable ragù and tossed with roasted-potato dumplings. If you cannot find all of the vegetables, feel free to substitute extra onions or other root vegetables.

*Pair with*
AN AGED
WHITE WINE

We like: Kalin Cellars Semillon—or choose your most comforting drink to accompany this comfort food.

## SERVES 4 TO 6

2 chicken legs (about 1 pound)

1 teaspoon kosher salt, plus more for seasoning

Freshly cracked black pepper

¼ cup extra-virgin olive oil

½ cup small dice Spanish or yellow onion

½ cup small dice carrot

½ cup small dice celery

½ cup small dice celery root

½ cup small dice fennel

½ cup small dice parsnip

2 sprigs fresh thyme

1 bay leaf

1 cup dry white wine, such as Pinot Grigio

1¼ cups chicken stock

Gnocchi (recipe follows)

4 tablespoons unsalted butter

3 fresh sage leaves, torn

3 tablespoons freshly grated Parmesan cheese, plus more for garnish

Preheat the oven to 300°F. Season the chicken legs generously with salt and pepper. Heat a large sauté pan or cast-iron skillet over high heat. Add 2 tablespoons of the olive oil. When the oil is hot, gently place the chicken legs in the pan, skin side down. Cook the chicken undisturbed until the skin is brown and the chicken releases easily from the pan, 4 to 6 minutes. Turn the chicken over and brown the other side, 3 to 4 minutes more. Remove the chicken from the pan and set aside on a plate while making the braising mixture.

In a medium (3-quart) ovenproof saucepan, place the remaining 2 tablespoons olive oil, the onion, carrot, celery, celery root, fennel, parsnip, thyme, bay leaf, and the 1 teaspoon salt over high heat. Cook, stirring frequently, until all of the vegetables are soft and they start to take on a slight golden color, about 10 minutes. Add the white wine and cook until the wine has completely evaporated, 5 to 6 minutes. Add 1 cup of the chicken stock to the pan. Bring the contents of the pan to a boil and turn off the heat. Add the chicken legs to the braising mixture, cover the pan, and place in the oven. Braise the chicken for 50 to 60 minutes, until the meat is tender and easily releases from the bone. Check the meat in several places with a metal skewer or fork; the skewer or fork should easily slide into the meat.

# GNOCCHI WITH BRAISED CHICKEN
## CONTINUED

Remove from the oven and place the chicken legs on a cutting board. Increase the oven temperature to 350°F. Line a baking sheet with parchment paper.

Return the saucepan to the stovetop. Cook the sauce over medium heat until most of the liquid has evaporated and the mixture is a thick ragù, 20 to 25 minutes.

Meanwhile, remove the chicken skin from the legs. Lay the chicken skin flat on the prepared baking sheet. Place in the oven and roast the chicken skin until it is a deep golden brown color, 20 to 30 minutes. Remove from the oven and let cool for 15 to 20 minutes, until cool enough to touch with your hands. Finely mince the browned chicken skin and add the skin to the braising mixture.

Remove all of the chicken meat from the bones. Discard any tendons. Cut the meat into ½-inch pieces and add to the braise. Taste the ragù and add more salt, if necessary. The chicken ragù can be made ahead to this point and stored in an airtight container in the refrigerator for 3 to 4 days or in the freezer for 2 weeks.

To prepare the gnocchi, bring a large pot of water to a boil. Season the water generously with salt.

Meanwhile, in a large sauté pan, place 2 tablespoons of the butter over high heat. Cook until the butter starts to turn brown, about 1 minute. Add the sage leaves. Cook for a minute or two until the butter is brown and the sage leaves are crispy. Add the chicken ragù and the remaining ¼ cup chicken stock to the pan. Bring the ragù to a simmer, then reduce the heat to low while cooking the gnocchi.

Cook the gnocchi in 2 or 3 batches, depending on the size of the pot. If the gnocchi are too crowded, they will stick together and they won't cook evenly. Add the gnocchi to the water and gently stir. After the gnocchi float to the top of the water, let them continue to cook for another minute. Fresh gnocchi will cook in just 1 to 2 minutes. Use a slotted spoon or spatula to gently remove the gnocchi from the water and add them to the sauce. Gently stir into the sauce, making sure the gnocchi do not stick together. Continue with the next batch or two of gnocchi.

Add the remaining 2 tablespoons butter, the 3 tablespoons Parmesan, and several turns of black pepper to the gnocchi and sauce. Stir gently, simmering 1 to 2 minutes more to thicken as needed. Otherwise, serve immediately in warm bowls. Garnish with extra grated Parmesan, if desired.

# GNOCCHI

Gnocchi is usually made with boiled potatoes, but I prefer roasted potatoes instead. This eliminates any excess moisture and gives the gnocchi even more intense potato flavor. The trick with gnocchi is to refrain from over-kneading the dough. As soon as the mixture holds together, it is ready to form into dumplings. Also, be sure to cook them on the day that they are made—if they sit in the refrigerator overnight, they will discolor. Don't freeze them; frozen gnocchi have a tendency to explode in boiling water. This recipe makes about 80 pieces.

## SERVES 4 TO 6

3 large russet baking potatoes (about 1¾ pounds)

1⅔ cups (7 ounces) unbleached all-purpose flour, plus more for dusting

1 extra-large egg, beaten

1 teaspoon kosher salt

**SPECIAL EQUIPMENT**

- POTATO RICER

- BENCH KNIFE (PIE SCRAPER)

Preheat the oven to 350°F. Place the potatoes on a baking sheet and bake until the potatoes are thoroughly cooked and easily pierced with a metal skewer or fork, about 1 hour and 20 minutes. Let the potatoes cool for about 20 minutes, or until cool enough to handle.

Dust a clean baking sheet with flour and set aside.

With a paring knife, peel the skins from the potatoes and discard. Measure 1¼ pounds of the skinless cooked potatoes. Push the measured cooked potatoes through a ricer onto a large cutting board.

Sift the 1⅔ cups flour all over the riced potatoes. Drizzle the egg over the potato-flour mixture. Sprinkle with the salt. Using a bench knife (pie scraper) or your hands, gently fold the mixture together, constantly scraping the cutting board and turning the dough over to gently knead it together. Do not overmix.

Once the dough is homogeneous throughout, divide the ball into 4 equal pieces. Dust the pieces with flour. Working with 1 piece at a time, gently roll the dough with your hands into a long, ½-inch-thick log. Cut the log into 1-inch pieces. Using your thumb, press each piece of gnocchi into the tines of a fork and roll the dough off the fork. One side of the dough will be grooved from the fork tines and the other side will be indented from your thumb. Place the gnocchi on the prepared baking sheet. Continue this process with the rest of the dough.

The gnocchi can be stored, uncovered, on the prepared baking sheet in the refrigerator for several hours, but should be cooked the day they are made.

# PIZZOCCHERI WITH BRUSSELS SPROUTS, POTATOES, AND FONTINA

Pizzoccheri is a classic dish in Valtellina, the part of Italy that borders Switzerland. This is a hearty, soul-satisfying pasta that's perfect for the winter months, traditionally made with short, flat buckwheat noodles and tossed with cabbage, potatoes, and Valtellina casera cheese. Instead of cabbage, I use Brussels sprouts, with the more commonly found fontina cheese. We once had an Italian guest at L'Artusi complain that this dish was nothing like what his grandmother made. I don't doubt that. But I would hope that if I had an Italian grandmother, she would serve this dish to me.

*Pair with*
A DRY, EARTHY
HARD CIDER

This autumnal dish calls for apple notes, and the bubbles will cleanse your palate. We like: Domaine Dupont Organic Cider.

## SERVES 4 TO 6

| | | |
|---|---|---|
| 4 cups medium dice peeled Yukon gold potatoes | 8 large Brussels sprouts (about 8 ounces) | 1 cup chicken or vegetable stock |
| 2 tablespoons extra-virgin olive oil | 4 tablespoons unsalted butter | 11 ounces buckwheat pasta noodles (see page 109) |
| ½ teaspoon kosher salt, plus more for seasoning | 2 shallots, julienned | ½ cup freshly grated Parmesan cheese |
| Freshly cracked black pepper | 1 tablespoon plus 1 teaspoon thinly sliced fresh sage leaves | 4 ounces fontina cheese, diced |

Preheat the oven to 350°F. In a large bowl, toss together the diced potatoes, olive oil, the ½ teaspoon salt, and several turns of black pepper. Spread the potatoes onto a baking sheet. Place in the oven and roast until the potatoes are tender and slightly golden brown, 30 to 35 minutes.

Slice the bottoms off the Brussels sprouts. Peel off the outer leaves and discard. Continue peeling off the inner leaves, one by one, and set aside.

Place 2 tablespoons of the butter in a large sauté pan and place over high heat. Cook the butter undisturbed until the butter starts to turn golden brown, 1 to 2 minutes. Add the shallots and sage and season with a generous pinch of salt and a few turns of black pepper. Sauté the shallots and sage for 2 minutes. Add the Brussels sprout leaves and season them with a pinch or two of salt. Then add the roasted potatoes. Toss together and sauté the mixture for 1 minute. Add the stock and bring to a boil. Turn the heat down to low and cook until the liquid reduces by half, 5 to 6 minutes. Keep the sauce on low heat while cooking the noodles.

# PIZZOCCHERI WITH BRUSSELS SPROUTS, POTATOES, AND FONTINA
**CONTINUED**

Meanwhile, bring a large pot of water to a boil. Season the water generously with salt. Place the buckwheat noodles in the boiling water. Cook the noodles for 2 minutes, or until the pasta is just al dente. Taste a noodle to make sure that it is tender, but still chewy in the center. Use a slotted spoon or spatula to transfer the noodles to the Brussels sprout mixture. Reserve the pasta water.

Toss the noodles with the Brussels sprout sauce. Add the remaining 2 tablespoons butter and the grated Parmesan. Gently toss everything to combine. Let the noodles cook in the sauce for a minute or so. If there does not appear to be enough sauce for the noodles, add a tablespoon or two of pasta water. If it appears to be too loose, simmer for another minute or so. Taste the sauce and add a little more salt or pepper, if desired. Just before serving, toss the diced fontina into the pasta. The fontina should melt slightly, but still remain recognizable. Distribute the pasta among warm bowls and serve immediately.

# SPAGHETTI WITH TOMATO AND SHRIMP

This dish is easy to prepare and cooks in no time at all (the shrimp is briefly sautéed in a simple tomato sauce and tossed with spaghetti), making it a great last-minute supper. My favorite part is the Parmesan-panko breadcrumbs sprinkled on top. Although you won't find cheese and fish together in most Italian recipes, I personally love the taste of Parmesan with seafood; plus the breadcrumbs add a great crunchy texture to each bite.

*Pair with*
VERY CRISP
COASTAL
WHITE WINE

We like: Bisson Vermentino—
the brininess complements the
shrimp and its acidity stands up
to the tomato sauce.

## SERVES 4

½ cup panko (Japanese breadcrumbs)

2 tablespoons freshly grated Parmesan cheese

1 tablespoon finely chopped fresh flat-leaf parsley

⅛ teaspoon kosher salt, plus more for seasoning

¼ cup extra-virgin olive oil

8 garlic cloves, thinly sliced

1 tablespoon fresh oregano leaves

2 cups canned crushed Italian tomatoes, with juice

¼ teaspoon red chili flakes, plus more as needed

12 ounces dried spaghetti

10 to 12 ounces (16/20 count) shrimp, peeled, deveined, halved from head to tail, then halved crosswise

Preheat the oven to 350°F. Spread the panko on a baking sheet or in an ovenproof skillet. Place in the oven to toast for about 4 minutes. Stir and continue baking until golden brown, about 4 minutes more. Transfer the hot breadcrumbs to a bowl. Stir in the Parmesan, parsley, and the ⅛ teaspoon salt. The Parmesan will melt slightly and coat the breadcrumbs. Set the breadcrumbs aside and let cool to room temperature. Store in an airtight container at room temperature. The breadcrumbs can be prepared several days in advance.

Place 2 tablespoons of the olive oil, the garlic, oregano leaves, and a generous pinch of salt in a large sauté pan or Dutch oven. Cook over medium-high heat, stirring frequently, until the edges of the garlic start to turn golden brown, about 2 minutes.

Immediately add the tomatoes, chili flakes, and another generous pinch of salt. Decrease the heat to medium-low and simmer for 8 to 10 minutes. Taste the sauce and add more salt or chili flakes if necessary. The sauce should be slightly spicy. Keep the sauce warm over low heat.

# SPAGHETTI WITH TOMATO AND SHRIMP
## CONTINUED

Meanwhile, bring a large pot of water to a boil. Season generously with salt. Add the spaghetti and cook until just al dente, slightly less than the suggested cooking time on the package. Reserve the pasta water.

Meanwhile, a minute before the pasta is done, add the shrimp to the tomato sauce, season with a pinch of salt, and stir to combine. Using a slotted spoon or tongs, add the pasta and the remaining 2 tablespoons olive oil. Simmer over medium-low heat until the shrimp is cooked through, 1 to 2 minutes, thinning the sauce with pasta water as needed. Taste and adjust the seasoning.

Serve in warm bowls and garnish with a generous sprinkle of the toasted Parmesan panko crumbs.

# LINGUINI AND CLAMS WITH CHORIZO AND CHILI

Usually linguini with clams is made with bacon—and you can't go wrong with bacon. But I like to serve it with Spanish chorizo, which has a smokiness that works well with the briny clams. Please note that this recipe only serves 2 people. This is one of those dishes that doesn't multiply well—the sauce gets too thin and doesn't coat the noodles thoroughly. However, if you want to increase the recipe, you can serve the clams and sauce in bowls with grilled bruschetta on the side, as you would mussels (use a spoon to devour the sauce). Otherwise, consider this the perfect dish for Valentine's Day.

*Pair with*
GERMAN-STYLE ALE

To balance the chili in the dish, choose something refreshing and cooling. We like: Captain Lawrence Captain's Kölsch.

## SERVES 2

¼ cup small dice yellow onion

¼ cup small dice fennel

¼ cup small dice celery

2 tablespoons extra-virgin olive oil

Kosher salt

1 ounce Spanish chorizo or pepperoni, thinly sliced into half-moons

1 fresh hot red chili pepper (such as red jalapeño), thinly sliced, with seeds

1 tablespoon thinly sliced garlic, preferably sliced on a mandoline

1 tablespoon fresh oregano leaves

1 pound littleneck clams, scrubbed clean

¼ cup dry white wine, such as Pinot Grigio

6 ounces dried linguini

Freshly squeezed juice of ½ lemon

1 teaspoon unsalted butter

3 tablespoons chopped fresh flat-leaf parsley

1 tablespoon high-quality extra-virgin olive oil

Place the onion, fennel, celery, 1 tablespoon of the olive oil, and a generous pinch of salt in a large sauté pan over medium-high heat. Sauté, stirring frequently, until the vegetables are soft and begin to take on a slight golden color, 5 to 7 minutes. Transfer the sautéed vegetables to a small bowl and set aside.

Return the sauté pan to the heat and add the remaining 1 tablespoon olive oil. When the oil is hot, add the chorizo, chili, garlic, oregano leaves, and another generous pinch of salt. Sauté until the garlic begins to turn golden brown on the edges, 2 to 3 minutes. When the garlic starts to brown, add the sautéed vegetables and the clams. Toss to combine. Add the white wine, immediately cover the pan, and increase the heat to high. Cook undisturbed until the clams have opened, 5 to 7 minutes. Remove the cover and turn off the heat while waiting for the pasta to cook. Discard any clams that did not open. Taste and adjust the seasoning as needed.

Meanwhile, bring a large pot of water to a boil. Season the water generously with salt. Boil the pasta until just al dente, slightly less than the suggested cooking time on the package. Bite into a piece of linguini to make sure there is a small white dot in the center of the pasta. The pasta will finish cooking in the sauce.

Increase the heat under the clams to medium. Add the pasta to the clams and toss together. Add the lemon juice, butter, parsley, and high-quality olive oil. Toss together. Cook the contents of the pan for 1 to 2 minutes, until the sauce sufficiently coats the linguini. Divide the pasta between 2 warm serving bowls and distribute the clams on top of the pasta. Serve immediately, with a bowl alongside for the clamshells.

# PORK MEATBALLS WITH POLENTA

In L'Apicio's kitchen you will find a hilariously tacky trophy with plastic meatballs on the top. Yes, this is an award-winning recipe: "Best Meatballs" at the 2012 Meatball Madness, sponsored by the New York City Wine and Food Festival. These meatballs are aggressively seasoned with decidedly non-Italian spices—smoked paprika and cumin. Whether or not they taste Italian, they deserve a trophy!

*Pair with*
A RYE BEER

Rye beer has more spiciness to it, which you want with a super flavorful dish like this. We like: Sixpoint Righteous Ale.

## SERVES 4 TO 6 (ABOUT 20 MEATBALLS)

2 tablespoons extra-virgin olive oil

1½ cups small dice yellow onions

2 teaspoons kosher salt

1 tablespoon cumin seeds

1 tablespoon fennel seeds

1 pound ground pork

¼ cup panko breadcrumbs

¼ cup grated Pecorino Romano cheese, plus more for garnish

2 tablespoons sweet smoked paprika

2 tablespoons chopped fresh flat-leaf parsley

1 teaspoon red chili flakes

1 recipe Amatriciana Sauce (see page 106)

Polenta (recipe follows)

High-quality extra-virgin olive oil

Preheat the oven to 350°F. In a small (2-quart) saucepan, place the olive oil, onions, and 1 teaspoon of the salt over medium-high heat. Cook, stirring the onions frequently, until the onions are slightly golden brown, about 15 minutes. Transfer the onions to a plate and let cool in the refrigerator, uncovered, for at least 30 minutes.

Place the cumin seeds and fennel seeds in a small sauté pan. Set the sauté pan over medium heat. Cook the spices, tossing them frequently, until fragrant and aromatic, 1 to 2 minutes. Finely grind the toasted spices in a spice grinder. Place the spices in a large bowl. Add the ground pork, breadcrumbs, the ¼ cup Pecorino, the smoked paprika, parsley, chili flakes, the remaining 1 teaspoon salt, and the cooled onions. Using your hands, mash the mixture thoroughly to evenly distribute the ingredients throughout the pork. Using an ice cream scoop or your hands, form the meat mixture into 1¼-ounce (1¼- to 1½-inch) balls. Distribute the meatballs on a baking sheet, leaving space between them, and bake until browned on the outside, with an internal temperature of 170°F, about 20 minutes.

While the meatballs are in the oven, place the amatriciana sauce in a Dutch oven. Bring the sauce to a boil over medium-high heat, then reduce the heat to low. Add the roasted meatballs to the hot sauce. Toss to combine. Let the meatballs simmer in the sauce for 5 minutes.

Place the polenta in individual warm bowls or spread out onto a large platter (see Note). Scatter the meatballs and a generous amount of the sauce on the polenta. Garnish with freshly grated Pecorino Romano and a drizzle of high-quality olive oil.

**NOTE:** The classic Italian preparation, *polenta alla spianatora,* calls for the polenta to be "spread flat" on a board; that's how we serve it at L'Apicio, and you may like to do the same. Spreading cools the polenta, making it easier to divide and serve—but if you like your polenta piping hot, it's better to serve it in individual warm bowls.

# POLENTA

If you cook polenta on the stove, it requires constant stirring to prevent it from scorching on the bottom of the pan. Maybe I'm lazy, but constantly stirring polenta is not for me. I prefer to cook polenta, covered, in the oven—it cooks more evenly and there's no concern about burning the dish. Any leftover polenta can be reheated (just whisk in some water and get the mixture good and hot) or cut into squares and grilled or fried.

## MAKES JUST OVER 1 QUART

4 cups water

1 cup polenta
(not instant)

1 teaspoon kosher salt,
plus more as needed

½ cup grated
Parmesan cheese

1 tablespoon
unsalted butter

1 tablespoon extra-
virgin olive oil

Preheat the oven to 350°F. Place the water, polenta, and ½ teaspoon of the salt in a medium (3-quart) ovenproof saucepan with a lid. Over medium heat on the stovetop, bring the contents of the saucepan to a simmer, stirring frequently. Cover. Place in the oven and bake for 30 to 40 minutes. Taste the polenta to make sure that it is completely cooked and not raw-tasting. Whisk in the Parmesan, butter, olive oil, and the remaining ½ teaspoon salt. Taste and add more salt if needed. Serve hot.

If serving in an hour or two, cover the polenta with a lid and keep in a warm oven (250°F) until ready to serve. Alternatively, you can reheat the polenta over medium heat on the stovetop. Add some water (about ¼ cup) to loosen the polenta and whisk constantly while reheating to smooth out the consistency and to prevent the polenta from scorching on the bottom of the pan.

# SWEET CORN MEZZALUNA

When Erin Shambura started working at L'Artusi as my chef de cuisine, she spearheaded the idea of offering a seasonal ravioli on the menu. In the summer, Erin makes an incredible corn mezzaluna (half-moon-shaped ravioli). Sweet corn is not commonly found in Italy, but when simply sautéed and pureed with ricotta, it makes a deliciously sweet and delicate ravioli filling. Mezzaluna are easy to form and have the perfect filling-to-noodle ratio. Do not be intimidated by this recipe—the filling can be made in advance, and once you have made the first few ravioli, the rest are easy to execute. This recipe makes enough mezzaluna for about 6 servings; only boil as many as you want for now and the rest will freeze beautifully.

*Pair with*
WHITE WINE
OR BEER

Choose a rich, full white or a golden, flavorful beer. We like: La Castellada Ribolla Gialla or Victory Helios Ale.

## SERVES 4

### FILLING AND MEZZALUNA (MAKES 35 TO 40 MEZZALUNA)

2 tablespoons extra-virgin olive oil

1 tablespoon unsalted butter

1 large shallot, peeled and finely chopped

Kosher salt

2 cups fresh or frozen corn kernels

1 cup ricotta

¼ cup freshly grated Parmesan cheese

Unbleached all-purpose flour

Egg Yolk Pasta Dough (page 110)

### LEMON-BUTTER SAUCE AND COOKING THE MEZZALUNA

Kosher salt

6 tablespoons unsalted butter

1 teaspoon finely grated lemon zest

½ teaspoon freshly cracked black pepper

20 to 24 mezzaluna

1 tablespoon freshly grated Parmesan, plus more for garnish

## SPECIAL EQUIPMENT

- PASTA MACHINE
- PASTRY BRUSH
- PIPING BAG
- 2½ TO 3-INCH BISCUIT CUTTER

To make the corn filling, heat the olive oil and butter over medium heat in a large sauté pan. Add the shallot and season generously with salt. Sauté until the shallot is soft, about 2 minutes. Add the corn kernels and another generous pinch of salt. Sauté for 4 to 5 minutes, until the corn is tender.

Place the corn mixture, the ricotta, and Parmesan in a food processor. Process until smooth, periodically scraping down the sides of the bowl. Set the mixture aside in a large bowl. Taste, and add more salt if necessary. The filling can be made ahead and stored in an airtight container for 3 days in the refrigerator or for 2 weeks in the freezer (let thaw for 2 hours at room temperature or overnight in the refrigerator before using).

# SWEET CORN MEZZALUNA
## CONTINUED

To assemble the mezzaluna, dust a large baking sheet with flour and set aside. Divide the pasta dough into 4 pieces. Working with 1 piece at a time, dust the dough with flour. Roll through a pasta machine at the largest setting. Decrease the thickness setting by 1 notch and roll the dough through again. Continue decreasing the setting and rolling the pasta until it has gone through the second-to-last setting (at this point the pasta will be thin and should be handled carefully). Cover the rolled-out sheet of pasta with plastic wrap to keep it pliable while rolling the remaining sheets. Repeat the entire process with the remaining 3 pieces of dough.

Lightly brush 1 large sheet of pasta with water. Spoon the filling into a piping bag or a plastic bag with 1 corner trimmed off. With the long edge of 1 sheet of pasta facing you, use the bag to pipe 1 heaping teaspoon of corn filling every 2 inches horizontally across the center of the sheet of pasta. Fold the top half of the pasta sheet over the bottom half of the pasta sheet. Press the air out between the mounds of filling and pinch the dough together. Work from the middle out to remove any air pockets.

Using a biscuit cutter, cut around the pockets of corn filling to make half-moon shapes. Crimp the rounded edges with the tines of a fork. Set the completed mezzaluna on the floured baking sheet. Repeat with the 3 remaining pasta sheets (discard any dough scraps). Store on the baking sheet in the refrigerator until ready to cook.

To make the lemon-butter sauce and cook the pasta, bring a large pot of water to a boil. Season generously with salt.

Place a large sauté pan over medium heat. Add the butter, 3 tablespoons of the boiling water, the lemon zest, pepper, and a pinch or two of salt. Swirl to combine. Do not let the mixture come to a simmer. Decrease the heat to low.

Add the mezzaluna to the boiling water and boil for 2 to 3 minutes, until they float in the water. Using a spider or slotted spoon, gently transfer the mezzaluna to the lemon-butter sauce. Add the 1 tablespoon grated Parmesan. Stir together gently and turn the mezzaluna over to coat them in the sauce. Taste and adjust the seasoning if necessary. Serve in warm bowls with additional freshly grated Parmesan.

PRIMI

# TAJARIN ALLA CARBONARA

This dish combines two classic elements from two different regions of Italy. Tajarin is an egg yolk–based noodle traditionally served in Piedmont with truffles. Carbonara is a Roman dish that incorporates bacon, cheese, and black pepper (never scallions, but I like them). The carbonara sauce is thickened by gently heating an egg yolk in the mixture. My former chef de cuisine at dell'anima, Mike Berardino, preferred to serve the egg yolk raw on top of the pasta, so guests can toss the yolk into the dish and create their own sauce.

*Pair with*
A FULL WHITE
OR DRY RED

Choose an earthy white or a smoky red. We like: Graci Etna Bianco "Quota 600" or Tenuta delle Terre Nere Etna Rosso.

**SERVES 4 TO 6**

- 4 tablespoons unsalted butter
- 4 ounces speck (see Note) or prosciutto, thinly sliced and cut into 1-inch pieces
- 8 scallions, outer leaves removed, thinly sliced

- 2 teaspoons freshly cracked black pepper
- ½ cup chicken stock, vegetable stock, or water
- Kosher salt

- 12 ounces tajarin (see page 110)
- 3 tablespoons freshly grated Pecorino Romano cheese, plus more for garnish
- 4 to 6 large eggs, at room temperature

Place 2 tablespoons of the butter, the speck, scallions, and pepper in a large sauté pan over high heat. Sauté for 2 to 3 minutes, until the speck is slightly crispy on the edges and starts to turn a light golden brown. Add the stock and simmer until the liquid reduces by half, about 2 minutes. Turn the heat to low while cooking the pasta.

Meanwhile, bring a large pot of water to a boil. Season the water generously with salt. Place the tajarin in the boiling water and cook until just al dente, 1 to 2 minutes. Taste the pasta to make sure it is slightly chewy in the center. Transfer the pasta from the boiling water to the sauce and toss together. Add the remaining 2 tablespoons butter and the 3 tablespoons grated Pecorino. Toss the ingredients together on low heat until the butter melts into the sauce.

Distribute the pasta among warm serving bowls. Working over a clean bowl, crack 1 egg and separate the yolk from the white. Carefully place the yolk on top of 1 pasta serving. Repeat with the remaining eggs and pasta servings. (Discard the egg whites or save for another use.) Crack some black pepper over each yolk. Garnish each serving with additional grated cheese. Serve immediately.

**NOTE:** Speck is an Italian smoked prosciutto from Alto Adige. If it's unavailable, regular prosciutto, bacon, or pancetta can be used instead.

# RIGATONI WITH ROASTED BUTTERNUT SQUASH AND BACON

I have my dear friend Sal Rizzo to thank for this dish, which he made for one of his Sunday suppers. I begged Sal to let me steal his idea. My version uses bacon instead of sausage, and walnuts seemed to add just the right amount of texture.

*Pair with*
A CRISP
WHITE WINE

We like: Keuka Lake Vineyards "Falling Man" Riesling: dry, but a little sweet.

## SERVES 4 TO 6

- 4 cups butternut squash cut into "batons" (½ by ½ by 1½ inches) or large dice
- ¼ cup extra-virgin olive oil
- ½ teaspoon kosher salt, plus more for seasoning
- Freshly cracked black pepper
- 3 tablespoons unsalted butter
- 4 ounces thick-cut bacon, cut into ¼-inch slices
- 10 fresh sage leaves, torn
- 2 shallots, julienned
- ½ cup dry white wine, such as Pinot Grigio
- ½ cup chicken stock
- 10 ounces dried rigatoni
- 2 tablespoons grated Pecorino Romano cheese
- 6 tablespoons roughly chopped walnuts

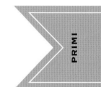

PRIMI

Preheat the oven to 350°F. In a large bowl, toss the squash with 2 tablespoons of the olive oil, the ½ teaspoon salt, and several turns of pepper. Spread the squash on a baking sheet. Roast until the squash is tender, but still holds its shape, about 30 minutes. Use a metal spatula to gently loosen the roasted squash from the pan. Set aside.

Place a large sauté pan over medium-high heat. Add 1 tablespoon of the olive oil and 1 tablespoon of the butter. When the butter mixture begins to turn slightly brown (2 to 3 minutes), add the bacon. Cook the bacon, stirring frequently, until the fat starts to render and the bacon starts to brown, 3 to 5 minutes. Add the sage and shallots. Sauté for 3 to 5 minutes, until the shallots start to soften and caramelize. Add the roasted squash and sauté for 1 to 2 minutes more. Add the white wine and cook until it evaporates completely, about 2 minutes. Add the stock and simmer for 2 minutes. Decrease the heat to very low and keep the sauce warm until the pasta is ready.

Meanwhile, bring a large pot of water to a boil. Season the water generously with salt. Cook the rigatoni until just al dente, slightly less than the suggested cooking time on the package. The pasta should have a small white line in the center.

Transfer the pasta from the water to the sauce. Reserve the pasta water. Increase the heat under the sauce to medium and add the remaining 1 tablespoon olive oil and 2 tablespoons butter, the Pecorino, and the walnuts. Stir to combine. Cook for another minute or so. Thin the sauce with pasta water or simmer for 1 to 2 minutes more to thicken as needed. Serve in warm bowls.

# SAUSAGE AND PEPPERS WITH POLENTA

To me, this is the quintessential New York Italian-American comfort dish, as a walk through the San Gennaro festival in Little Italy will demonstrate. I like to roast the peppers and tomatoes in the oven and then toss them into a sausage ragù. Polenta is the perfect way to soak up the sauce, but the combination is also great served as a sandwich on a crusty roll or tossed with orecchiette.

*Pair with*
A CRISP, SOUR BEER

Sausage and peppers is beer food. Italy has many interesting small-production beers—choose your favorite. We like: Baladin "Nora" Sour.

**SERVES 4 TO 6**

1 pound red and yellow bell peppers, stems and seeds removed, sliced into ½-inch-thick strips

2 cups (8 ounces) cherry or grape tomatoes

6 tablespoons extra-virgin olive oil

8 sprigs fresh thyme

2 teaspoons kosher salt

1 pound spicy Italian sausage, casings removed

2 cups small dice yellow onions

1 tablespoon fresh oregano leaves

1 tablespoon tomato paste

½ cup dry white wine, such as Pinot Grigio

½ cup vinegar from hot pickled peppers (or ½ cup white distilled vinegar plus ⅛ teaspoon chili oil)

1 cup chicken stock

Polenta (page 95)

Preheat the oven to 350°F. Line a baking sheet with parchment paper. In a large bowl, toss together the peppers, tomatoes, 2 tablespoons of the olive oil, the thyme sprigs, and 1 teaspoon of the salt. Spread the pepper mixture out on the prepared baking sheet and roast for 35 minutes, or until the peppers are soft and slightly charred on the edges. Discard the thyme sprigs.

Meanwhile, heat 2 tablespoons of the olive oil in a large sauté pan over high heat. When the oil is hot, gently add half of the sausage meat to the pan. Using a wooden spoon, break the sausage into ½- to 1-inch chunks. Brown the sausage pieces on all sides, about 5 minutes. Using a slotted spoon, transfer the browned sausage to a plate and set aside. Add the remaining sausage and repeat this process.

Discard the oil from the hot pan, but do not clean the pan. Return the pan to the heat and add the remaining 2 tablespoons olive oil, the onions, oregano leaves, and the remaining 1 teaspoon salt. Sauté the onions, scraping the sausage bits from the bottom of the pan, until the onions are softened and slightly caramelized, about 5 minutes. Add the tomato paste. Cook, constantly scraping the bottom of the pan, until the paste is slightly browned, about 2 minutes. Return the sausage to the pan and cook for 2 to 3 minutes. Add the white wine and vinegar. Cook until the liquid evaporates completely, 5 to 7 minutes. Add the chicken stock and simmer until the liquid reduces by half, about 7 minutes. Add the roasted peppers and tomatoes. Toss to combine. Simmer over medium heat until the mixture looks like a thick stew, 8 to 10 minutes. The sausage-pepper sauce can be made ahead to this point and stored in an airtight container for 3 to 4 days in the refrigerator, or for 2 weeks in the freezer.

To serve, divide the polenta among the serving plates or spread onto a large platter (see Note, page 95). Distribute the sausage and pepper mixture over the polenta.

# WHOLE WHEAT SPAGHETTI WITH BROCCOLI RABE PESTO

This dish came about while I was rummaging through our refrigerator at home. Broccoli rabe and olives are a perfect match, and the almonds complement the nuttiness of the whole wheat pasta. Unlike most sauces, pesto is best tossed with pasta when it's at room temperature, as the pesto can sometimes discolor and separate when too much heat is applied. Any leftover pesto can be spread on sandwiches or bruschetta.

*Pair with*
A CRISP,
FLAVORFUL
WHITE

We like: Red Hook Winery's Sauvignon Blanc, made with grapes from Macari Vineyards—a full-bodied, food-friendly wine.

## SERVES 4 TO 6

| | | |
|---|---|---|
| Kosher salt | 2 tablespoons chopped kalamata olives | ¼ cup plus 2 tablespoons extra-virgin olive oil |
| ½ bunch broccoli rabe | | |
| ¼ cup whole almonds | 2 tablespoons grated Parmesan cheese | 12 ounces fresh whole wheat spaghetti (see page 111), or dried |
| 2 garlic cloves | | |

Preheat the oven to 350°F. Bring a large pot of water to a boil. Season the water generously with salt. Trim the bottom ends (1 inch) off the broccoli rabe. Blanch the broccoli rabe in the boiling water for 2 to 3 minutes, until it turns bright green and the stems are tender. Drain the broccoli rabe and spread it out on a cooling rack; let cool to room temperature, 15 to 20 minutes.

Meanwhile place the almonds on a baking sheet and roast in the oven until toasted and aromatic, about 7 minutes. Allow to cool for 5 to 10 minutes.

Roughly chop the broccoli rabe and measure 1 cup of the cooked vegetable. In a food processor, pulse the toasted almonds with the garlic until finely chopped. Add the cup of broccoli rabe, the olives, and Parmesan. With the food processor running, slowly pour in the ¼ cup olive oil. Scrape down the sides of the bowl with a rubber spatula. Continue processing for 30 seconds to 1 minute. The contents should look like a bright green paste. Taste and add a pinch of salt if necessary. If the broccoli rabe was blanched in sufficiently salty water, the mixture should not need any more salt.

To make the pasta, bring another large pot of water to a boil. Season the water generously with salt. Add the pasta to the boiling water. Cook to desired doneness, 1 to 3 minutes if using fresh pasta. Reserve the pasta water.

Meanwhile, place 6 tablespoons of the pesto and the 2 tablespoons olive oil in a large bowl. Add the spaghetti to the pesto along with ¼ cup of the pasta water. Toss to combine. If the pesto seems too stiff, add a little more pasta water. If you would like the noodles to be more heavily coated in pesto, add another tablespoon of pesto to the bowl. Distribute the pasta among warm serving bowls and serve immediately.

# BUCATINI ALL'AMATRICIANA

Without a doubt, this is my favorite pasta dish. Amatriciana is a classic Italian pasta sauce that's traditionally made with tomato, sautéed onions, and guanciale, or cured pork jowls. At the restaurants, we cure our own pork belly and use that, but at home I use bacon—deliciously smoky, always perfectly cured, and easier to find.

*Pair with*
A JUICY BUT SAVORY RED WINE

It should be full-bodied, not too dry, with good acidity. We like: Occhipinti il Frappato.

**SERVES 4 TO 6**

8 ounces bacon, small dice

2 cups small dice Spanish onions

1 teaspoon kosher salt, plus more for the pasta water

½ teaspoon red chili flakes

2 tablespoons tomato paste

1 (28-ounce) can crushed Italian tomatoes, with juice

1 bay leaf

14 ounces dried bucatini or spaghetti

2½ tablespoons extra-virgin olive oil

5 tablespoons freshly grated Pecorino Romano cheese, plus more for garnish

Place the bacon in a Dutch oven over high heat on the stovetop. Cook the bacon, stirring frequently, until the fat has rendered and the bacon starts to turn slightly brown and crispy, about 6 minutes. Add the onions, ½ teaspoon of the salt, and the chili flakes. Sauté until the onions start to caramelize slightly, about 7 minutes.

Add the tomato paste to the onions and bacon. Continue cooking, constantly scraping the bottom of the pan, until the tomato paste browns slightly, about 2 minutes.

Add the canned tomatoes, bay leaf, and the remaining ½ teaspoon salt. Bring to a boil, then decrease the heat to low. Simmer for 25 to 30 minutes, stirring occasionally and scraping down and incorporating any caramelized bits of sauce that cling to the sides of the pan (they will enrich the flavor of the sauce). Remove the bay leaf and discard. The sauce can be made a day or two in advance and kept refrigerated in an airtight container. If serving immediately, keep the sauce on low heat while cooking the pasta.

Meanwhile, bring a large pot of water to a boil. Season generously with salt. Add the bucatini and cook until just al dente, slightly less than the suggested cooking time on the package. Reserve the pasta water.

Transfer the bucatini to the amatriciana sauce. Add the olive oil, the 5 tablespoons grated Pecorino, and ½ cup of the pasta water. Stir together and simmer for 2 minutes, thinning the sauce with pasta water or simmering for 1 to 2 minutes more to thicken as needed. Serve in warm bowls and garnish with additional Pecorino.

# FRESH PASTA RECIPES

## BASIC PASTA (FOR GARGANELLI AND FARFALLE)

**MAKES 14 OUNCES**

2 cups unbleached
all-purpose flour,
plus more for
rolling the dough

3 extra-large eggs

½ teaspoon kosher salt

Semolina flour

Place the 2 cups flour, the eggs, and salt in a food processor. Process for 1 minute to combine the ingredients. Transfer the dough to a work surface and knead into a ball. Wrap the dough in plastic wrap and refrigerate for 30 minutes.

Divide the pasta dough into 2 pieces. Working with 1 piece at a time, dust the dough with all-purpose flour. Roll through a pasta machine at the largest setting. Dust again with flour. Fold the dough lengthwise into thirds. Roll through the machine again. Repeat this process 1 or 2 more times.

Decrease the thickness setting by 1 notch. Roll the dough through the machine. Repeat this process, gradually decreasing the thickness, until the pasta has gone through the second-to-last setting. Cover the rolled-out pasta with plastic wrap to keep it pliable. Repeat the entire process with the remaining piece of dough. Dust a baking sheet with semolina flour and set aside.

**TO MAKE GARGANELLI:** Cut each sheet of dough lengthwise in half. Then cut the strips into 2- by 2-inch squares. Lay the pasta squares diagonally so that you're looking at diamond shapes. Lightly wet the top corner of 1 diamond. Working from the bottom point to the top, loosely roll the diamond over a dowel or chopstick (or use your finger or a ballpoint pen). Press to seal at the end of the diamond. Gently remove the dowel from the pasta and place the pasta on the prepared baking sheet. Continue until all the pasta has been formed into little "quills." Store the garganelli, uncovered, in the refrigerator until ready to cook. If the pasta is not going to be served the same day, place the baking sheet in the freezer. Once the pasta is frozen solid (1 to 2 hours), transfer it to an airtight container. The garganelli can be stored in the freezer for up to 2 weeks.

**TO MAKE FARFALLE:** Cut each sheet of dough lengthwise in half. Then cut the strips into 2- by 2-inch squares. One square at a time, place your index finger in the center of the square. Using your thumb and second finger of the same hand, pinch the edges of the dough together toward the center, releasing your index finger as you squeeze the dough. Pinch the center of the dough together. The pasta should look like bow ties. Place the bow ties on the prepared baking sheet. Continue until all of the pasta has been formed into bow ties. Store the farfalle, uncovered, in the refrigerator until ready to cook. If the pasta is not going to be served the same day, place the baking sheet in the freezer. Once the pasta is frozen solid (1 to 2 hours), transfer it to an airtight container. The farfalle can be stored in the freezer for up to 2 weeks.

## SPINACH PASTA

**MAKES 20 OUNCES**

½ teaspoon kosher salt, plus more for cooking the spinach

5 ounces fresh spinach

½ tablespoon extra-virgin olive oil, plus more as needed

2¼ cups plus 2 tablespoons unbleached all-purpose flour, plus more for dusting

12 extra-large egg yolks

2 tablespoons plus 1 teaspoon semolina flour, plus more for dusting

Bring a large pot of water to a boil. Season the water generously with salt. Blanch the spinach for 30 seconds. Remove the spinach with a spider or slotted spoon. Place the cooked spinach on a cooling rack or on a plate lined with paper towels. Pat the spinach dry with paper towels.

Transfer the spinach and olive oil to a blender. Process until the spinach forms a thick puree. If the spinach or the machine is not cooperating, add a splash or two of olive oil or water to get the spinach to puree (but ideally you will have as little liquid as possible in the puree). Measure 6 tablespoons of spinach puree for the pasta dough. Discard the remaining puree or save it for another use.

To make the pasta dough, place the 6 tablespoons of spinach puree, the 2¼ cups plus 2 tablespoons all-purpose flour, the egg yolks, the 2 tablespoons plus 1 teaspoon semolina flour, and the ½ teaspoon salt in a food processor. Process for a minute to combine the ingredients. Transfer the ingredients to a work surface and knead into a ball. Wrap the dough in plastic wrap and refrigerate for 30 minutes.

Divide the pasta dough into 4 pieces. Working with 1 piece at a time, dust the dough with all-purpose flour. Roll through a pasta machine at the largest setting. Dust again with flour. Fold the dough lengthwise into thirds. Roll through the machine again. Repeat this process 1 or 2 more times.

Decrease the thickness setting by 1 notch. Roll the dough through the machine. Repeat this process, gradually decreasing the thickness until the pasta has gone through the second-to-last setting. Cover the rolled-out pasta with plastic wrap to keep it pliable. Repeat the entire process with the remaining 3 pieces of dough.

Dust a baking sheet with semolina flour and set aside.

**TO MAKE TAGLIATELLE:** Using a pizza cutter or knife, cut each sheet of dough crosswise every 11 inches down the length of the dough. Then cut each rectangle lengthwise into 1-inch-wide strips. You will end up with noodles that are 1 inch wide by 11 inches long. Toss the tagliatelle with semolina flour and set aside, bundled into little nests, on the prepared baking sheet. Store the tagliatelle, uncovered, in the refrigerator until ready to cook. If the pasta is not going to be served the same day, place the baking sheet in the freezer. Be sure to divide the pasta into nests with your desired portion size. If it is all in one mass, it will be impossible to divide once frozen. Once the pasta is frozen solid (1 to 2 hours), transfer it to an airtight container. The tagliatelle can be stored in the freezer for up to 2 weeks.

# BUCKWHEAT PASTA (FOR PIZZOCCHERI)
## MAKES 11 OUNCES

¾ cup unbleached all-purpose flour, plus more for dusting

¾ cup buckwheat flour

1 extra-large egg yolk

5 tablespoons whole milk

½ teaspoon kosher salt

Semolina flour

Place the all-purpose flour, buckwheat flour, egg yolk, milk, and salt in a food processor. Process for 1 minute to combine the ingredients. Transfer the dough to a work surface and knead into a ball. Wrap the dough in plastic wrap and refrigerate for 30 minutes.

Divide the pasta dough into 2 pieces. Working with 1 piece at a time, dust the dough with all-purpose flour and roll the pasta through a pasta machine at the largest setting. Decrease the thickness setting by 1 notch. Dust the dough again with flour. Roll the dough through the machine. Repeat this process, gradually decreasing the thickness until the pasta has gone through the third-to-last setting (setting #6). Cover the rolled-out pasta with plastic wrap to keep it pliable. Repeat the entire process with the remaining piece of dough.

Dust a baking sheet with semolina flour and set aside.

**TO MAKE PIZZOCCHERI:** Using a pizza cutter or knife, cut each sheet of dough crosswise every 6 inches down the length of the dough. Then cut each rectangle lengthwise into 2-inch-wide strips. You will end up with noodles that are 2 inches wide by 6 inches long. Lay the buckwheat noodles flat onto the prepared baking sheet. Dust the noodles with semolina flour. If storing multiple layers of buckwheat noodles, place parchment paper between each layer and make sure the noodles are dusted with semolina on both sides. Store the buckwheat noodles, uncovered, in the freezer until ready to cook. If the pasta is not going to be served the same day, once the buckwheat noodles are frozen solid (1 to 2 hours), transfer to an airtight container. The noodles can be stacked on top of one another in the container. The pasta can be stored in the freezer for up to 2 weeks.

## FRESH PASTA RECIPES
**CONTINUED**

## EGG YOLK PASTA (FOR TAJARIN AND MEZZALUNA)
**MAKES 18 OUNCES**

2 cups unbleached
all-purpose flour

15 extra-large
egg yolks

½ teaspoon kosher salt

Semolina flour

Place the flour, egg yolks, and salt in a food processor. Process for 1 minute to combine the ingredients. Transfer the ingredients to a work surface and knead into a ball. Wrap the dough in plastic wrap and refrigerate for 30 minutes.

Divide the pasta dough into 4 pieces. Working with 1 piece of dough at a time, roll the dough through a pasta machine at the largest setting. Decrease the thickness setting by 1 notch. Roll the dough through the machine. Repeat this process, gradually decreasing the thickness until the pasta has gone through the second-to-last setting. Cover the rolled-out pasta with plastic wrap to keep it pliable. Repeat the entire process with the remaining 3 pieces of dough. Dust a baking sheet with semolina flour and set aside.

**TO MAKE TAJARIN:** Cut the 4 sheets of dough crosswise every 9 inches down the length of the dough. If your pasta machine has a fettuccini attachment, roll each rectangle through the attachment. Otherwise, roll up the rectangle jelly-roll style and cut the pasta into 1/4-inch-wide strips. Toss the tajarin with semolina and set aside, bundled into little nests, on the prepared baking sheet.

Store the tajarin, uncovered, in the refrigerator until ready to cook. If the pasta is not going to be served the same day, place the baking sheet in the freezer. Be sure to divide the pasta into nests with your desired portion size. (If it is all in one mass, it will be impossible to divide once frozen.) Once the pasta is frozen solid (1 to 2 hours), transfer to an airtight container. The tajarin can be stored in the freezer for up to 2 weeks.

**TO MAKE MEZZALUNA:** Follow the directions in the recipe on page 97.

# WHOLE WHEAT PASTA (FOR WHOLE WHEAT SPAGHETTI)

**MAKES 12 OUNCES**

1 cup whole
  wheat flour

1 cup semolina flour,
  plus more for dusting

3 extra-large eggs

½ teaspoon kosher salt

Place the whole wheat flour, the 1 cup semolina flour, the eggs, and salt in a food processor. Process for 1 minute to combine the ingredients. Transfer the ingredients to a work surface and knead into a ball. Wrap the dough in plastic wrap and refrigerate for 30 minutes.

Divide the pasta dough into 2 pieces. Working with 1 piece at a time, roll the dough through a pasta machine at the largest setting. Decrease the thickness setting by 1 notch. Roll the dough through the machine. Repeat this process, gradually decreasing the thickness until the pasta has gone through 4 times (the last setting should be #5). Cover the rolled-out pasta with plastic wrap to keep it pliable. Repeat the entire process with the remaining piece of dough.

Dust a baking sheet with semolina flour and set aside.

**TO MAKE WHOLE WHEAT SPAGHETTI:** Cut each sheet of dough crosswise every 9 inches down the length of the dough. Roll the rectangles through the spaghetti attachment on your pasta machine. Toss the spaghetti with the 1 cup semolina and set aside, bundled into little nests, on the prepared baking sheet. Store the spaghetti, uncovered, in the refrigerator until ready to cook. If the pasta is not going to be served the same day, place the sheet tray in the freezer. Be sure to divide the pasta into nests with your desired portion size. (If it is all in one mass, it will be impossible to divide once frozen.) Once the spaghetti is frozen solid (1 to 2 hours), transfer to an airtight container. The pasta can be stored in the freezer for up to 2 weeks.

*Chapter 4*

# SECONDI

It always seems as if restaurants have more interesting appetizers than they do main courses. Yet the main courses usually dominate the meal and the guests' experience. I like taking this challenge head-on. When creating a dish around a protein, I enjoy coming up with flavors and textures that make the dish memorable. I will select a protein and think about how it is best prepared—whether roasted, braised, or poached. Then, depending on the season and availability of ingredients, I pair the protein with a side dish that will bring out the flavors of the meat. Every once in a while I work in the opposite direction: Halfway through creating a vegetable dish, I realize it would be best complemented by a killer piece of meat. As long as the protein is cooked to perfection, sometimes all it needs is a sprinkle of Maldon sea salt flakes and a drizzle of high-quality olive oil to complete the dish. So how do you make sure it's perfect?

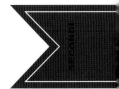

**SEASON MORE THAN YOU THINK.** It is important that the exterior of meat or fish be over-seasoned to compensate for the under-seasoned interior.

**LET THE PROTEIN SIT AT ROOM TEMPERATURE BEFORE COOKING.** Allow 30 minutes to 1 hour. This way, it will cook more evenly with less chance of overcooking.

**TAKE THE TEMPERATURE.** A digital thermometer registers the internal temperature of meat almost instantly and provides the most accurate way to tell if meat is properly cooked. Keep in mind that the internal temperature will continue to rise several degrees while resting.

**DON'T WALK AWAY.** Once protein gets to 100°F, it cooks very quickly. Keep an eye on the meat until it is ready.

**LET MEAT (NOT FISH) REST AT ROOM TEMPERATURE BEFORE SERVING.** This allows the meat to absorb all of its cooking liquid. If the meat is sliced too quickly after cooking, the juices run out and the meat tastes dry. In fact, serving meat at room temperature enhances the flavors.

**PLACE THE RESTING MEAT ON A BAKING SHEET LINED WITH A RACK.** This way air circulates evenly around it. If placed on a plate or cutting board, the meat will continue to cook on the bottom.

**INVEST IN A FEW HIGH-QUALITY INGREDIENTS**—particularly Maldon sea salt flakes and a high-quality olive oil (see page 71). And don't forget to use them!

*— Gabriel Thompson*

# DUCK BREASTS WITH RADICCHIO AND ROASTED TURNIPS

Duck breast is popularly served medium-rare. To me, it always seems too chewy and difficult to swallow at that temperature. But when duck breast is cooked a bit longer (medium is ideal), it is tender and delicious. Here the meat is served with roasted turnips, potatoes, and pears and drizzled with a honey-balsamic glaze. The bitterness of the charred radicchio counters the sweetness of the other ingredients. If you happen to have a bottle of Saba on hand, skip the balsamic glaze and instead drizzle a teaspoon of Saba over each dish before serving.

*Pair with*
AN ARTISANAL AMERICAN RED WINE

Choose one of the new reds made in the European style. We like: Trousseau from Arnot-Roberts—food-friendly, a little funky, easily drinkable.

## SERVES 4

- 12 ounces turnips, peeled, large dice
- 10 ounces Yukon gold potatoes, large dice
- 6 ounces pearl onions, halved (or cipollini onions, quartered)
- 2 Bartlett pears, stems and cores removed, large dice
- 3 tablespoons extra-virgin olive oil
- 1 tablespoon roughly chopped fresh rosemary
- 5 sprigs fresh thyme
- Kosher salt and freshly cracked black pepper
- 3 tablespoons balsamic vinegar
- 1½ tablespoons white distilled vinegar
- 1½ tablespoons honey
- 2 (7-ounce) duck breasts, at room temperature
- 1 head of radicchio, bottom trimmed, sliced into 4 wedges
- Maldon sea salt flakes (optional)

Preheat the oven to 400°F. In a large bowl, toss together the turnips, potatoes, onions, pears, olive oil, rosemary, and thyme. Season the vegetables aggressively with salt and pepper. Scatter the vegetables on a baking sheet or in a roasting pan. Place in the hot oven and roast until the vegetables are golden brown and tender, 35 to 45 minutes, turning the vegetables over midway through cooking. Remove from the oven and taste a couple of pieces of the roasted vegetables. If they seem under-seasoned, sprinkle the vegetables with additional salt. The vegetables can be made several hours in advance and rewarmed in a 350°F oven for 5 to 10 minutes before serving.

Place both vinegars and the honey in a small saucepan. Bring just to a simmer and stir to dissolve the honey, about 1 minute. Season with a pinch of salt. Pour the balsamic glaze into a small bowl and set aside at room temperature.

To cook the duck breasts, place a cast-iron skillet over medium-low heat. Lightly score the fat of the duck breasts with crosshatch marks about ½ inch by ½ inch. Season the duck breasts on both sides with salt and pepper. Place the duck breasts, fat side down, in the cast-iron skillet. Let the duck cook slowly until the fat renders and turns golden brown, about 20 minutes. Flip the breasts over and turn off the heat. Let the breasts sit in the pan until they have the proper internal temperature; for medium, remove the duck breasts when the internal temperature reaches 120°F (they will continue to cook while resting). Place the breasts on a baking sheet lined with a rack (leave the duck fat in the pan). Brush the breasts lightly with half the balsamic mixture and let rest while cooking the radicchio.

If the roasted vegetables need to be rewarmed, place them in the oven. Return the cast-iron skillet to medium-high heat. Place the radicchio wedges in the hot skillet. Cook the radicchio undisturbed until golden brown, 2 minutes. Turn the wedges over, sprinkle with salt and pepper, and cook for another 2 minutes. The radicchio should be golden brown on all sides.

Place 1 wedge of radicchio on each serving plate. Scatter the roasted vegetables on each plate. Slice the duck breasts into ¼-inch-thick slices and distribute among the plates. Drizzle 1 to 1½ teaspoons of balsamic glaze over each serving. Serve with Maldon sea salt flakes on the side, if desired.

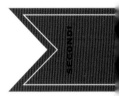

# CHICKEN AL DIAVOLO WITH BROCCOLI RABE

A chef I once worked for told me that other chefs judge you by your chicken. So when I was creating recipes for dell'anima, I decided that I wanted a dish that would have the oh-my-God-have-you-tried-this-chicken factor. I came up with this chicken *al diavolo* recipe. The name comes from *Fra Diavolo* (literally, "Brother Devil"), which is typically a spicy tomato-based sauce. My version is relatively spicy, but instead of tomato, the smoked paprika adds the red color that you would expect from the devil. This *diavolo* rub is also delicious on pork chops, quail, or catfish. I tried to take this dish off the menu once. Mayhem ensued. That's when I realized that I had succeeded in creating that perfect chicken dish.

*Pair with*
CHILLED RED
WINE OR A
FULL ROSÉ

We like: Torre dei Beati
"Cerasuolo d'Abruzzo"
Montepulciano.

**SERVES 2 TO 4**

1 (2½- to 3-pound) whole chicken

2½ tablespoons sweet smoked paprika (preferably Spanish)

1 tablespoon plus 1 teaspoon ground fennel seeds

1½ teaspoons red chili flakes

Kosher salt

2 tablespoons extra-virgin olive oil

1 cup chicken stock

2 teaspoons freshly squeezed lemon juice, plus more as needed

1 tablespoon high-quality extra-virgin olive oil

Broccoli Rabe with Garlic and Chilies (recipe follows)

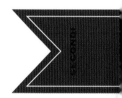

Preheat the oven to 350°F. Debone the chicken so that you end up with 2 sections, each with a breast, thigh, and leg (keep the skin on; see Notes). In a small bowl, combine the smoked paprika, ground fennel, and chili flakes. Generously season each chicken piece on both sides with salt. Then generously dust the chicken pieces on both sides with the smoked paprika mixture, using about 1 tablespoon of the spice rub for each half of the chicken.

Heat the olive oil in a large ovenproof sauté pan over medium-high heat. When hot, add the chicken, skin side down. Cook until the skin is golden brown and crispy, 4 to 5 minutes (see Notes). Place the sauté pan (still with the chicken skin side down) in the oven for 5 minutes. Turn the chicken over and return to the oven for 15 minutes more, or until the internal temperature reaches 155°F. Remove the chicken from the pan (do not clean the pan) and set the chicken aside on a rack at room temperature to rest.

# CHICKEN AL DIAVOLO WITH BROCCOLI RABE
**CONTINUED**

Return the sauté pan to the stovetop and add the chicken stock. Cook over medium-high heat, scraping the chicken bits off of the bottom of the pan, until the chicken stock is reduced by two-thirds (you should have ⅓ cup in the pan), about 5 minutes. Add the 2 teaspoons lemon juice and the high-quality olive oil. Taste and adjust the seasoning; it may need another pinch of salt or a dash of lemon juice.

Serve the chicken on a platter with the broccoli rabe. Generously spoon the chicken sauce around the serving platter.

**NOTES: Deboning chicken:** Using this method to debone a whole chicken helps flatten the white- and dark-meat pieces equally so that they can be cooked for the same amount of time. You can use boneless, skin-on chicken pieces in a pinch, but the thighs will take longer to cook. My deboning technique is different from the one many chefs use, but I find this method to be fast and straightforward.

1   Place the chicken breast side up on a cutting board, legs facing toward you.

2   Using a sharp chef's knife or deboning knife, cut along one side of the breastbone, following the contour to release the breast from the bone. Repeat along the other side of the breastbone.

3   Use your hands to bend back the leg and pop the leg joint (between the thigh and the body of the chicken).

4   Using the knife, cut between this joint and the body to release the thigh from the body. The breast should still be attached to the leg.

5   Cut the leg meat from the body. You will end up with a piece of chicken with a boneless breast and a leg with bones. Remove the backbone and rib cage and save for stock or discard.

6   Make an incision down the length of the leg bone.

7   Cut around all of the joints on the leg. Use the knife to scrape the meat away from the leg bone. Cut the bottom of the leg meat from the bottom of the leg bone.

8   Cut away any tendons in the leg meat. Cut away any extra fat and/or skin.

9   Cut off the wings and save for another use.

**Chicken skin:** For this dish, it is unbelievably important that the chicken skin be extra crispy. Let the chicken cook, skin side down, as long as possible before the spices start to burn. The fat will slowly render off of the skin and the results will be well worth it. Do not rush this process.

# BROCCOLI RABE WITH GARLIC AND CHILIES

This is Katherine's favorite side dish—she has it with every meal at all of our restaurants. Broccoli rabe has a slight bitterness to it that works well next to the smoked paprika in the Chicken *Al Diavolo*. When slicing the garlic, I use a Benriner Japanese mandoline, which produces paper-thin slices of garlic that are nearly translucent when they are cooked. Just be sure to slice the garlic very slowly and don't let your fingers get too close to the mandoline blade.

## SERVES 2 TO 4

Kosher salt

1 bunch broccoli rabe, stems trimmed by 1 inch

2 tablespoons extra-virgin olive oil

2 garlic cloves, very thinly sliced

1 pinch of red chili flakes, or more to taste

Line a baking sheet with paper towels. Bring a large pot of water to a boil. Season generously with salt. Taste the water; it should be super salty. Add the broccoli rabe and blanch until the broccoli is bright green and tender, 5 to 6 minutes. Remove the broccoli rabe from the cooking water and place it on the prepared baking sheet. Set it in the refrigerator for 15 to 20 minutes. The blanched broccoli rabe can be stored in an airtight container in the refrigerator for several hours.

Place the olive oil, garlic, a generous pinch of salt, and a pinch of chili flakes in a large sauté pan. Over medium heat, gently cook the garlic until just beginning to brown on the edges, 2 to 3 minutes. Add the broccoli rabe. Toss together and continue cooking until the broccoli rabe is hot. Taste and season with additional salt and chili flakes, if desired. Serve immediately with the chicken.

# GRILLED CORNISH HENS AL MATTONE

*Al mattone,* or "with a brick," is a classic cooking technique in Italy. With the backbone removed, the birds lie flat against the grill; the weight of the brick helps the birds cook faster and more evenly and ensures a crisp skin. If bricks are unavailable, a cast-iron skillet works well, too. The fennel-pepper dry rub is delicious; you may want to make extra and have it on hand to season steak, pork, or ribs before cooking.

*Pair with*
A FUNKY
ORANGE WINE

You want one that's as savory as the hens. We like: Anything Abe Schoener makes at the Scholium Project (scholiumwines.com) and Red Hook Winery.

**SERVES 4**

2 tablespoons whole fennel seeds

1 tablespoon mixed whole peppercorns (black, red, green, and white)

2 (1¾-pound) Cornish hens

Kosher salt

2 lemons, halved

4 teaspoons extra-virgin olive oil

**SPECIAL EQUIPMENT**

• 2 BRICKS

Preheat a grill to high; it should be piping hot. Grind the fennel seeds in a spice grinder and place in a small bowl. Finely grind the peppercorn mixture and add it to the bowl. Stir to combine.

To prepare the hens, use a chef's knife to cut out the wishbone, backbone, and wing tips. The bird should lie flat like a book. Remove and discard any excess fat and/or skin. Season the birds on both sides generously with salt. Then season both sides generously with the fennel-pepper rub, using about 1 tablespoon of the spice mixture for each bird.

Wrap 2 bricks individually with foil. Brush the cut side of each lemon half with 1 teaspoon of the oil.

Decrease the heat on the grill to medium. Place the hens on the grill, skin side down. Place a brick on each bird to weigh the bird down. Cook the hens undisturbed for 10 to 12 minutes. Remove the bricks. Use tongs to flip the birds over. Cook on the other side, without the weights, until the internal temperature reaches 150°F, 4 to 7 minutes more.

Meanwhile, when you flip the hens, place the lemons on the grill, cut side down. Cook on the grill until darkened grill marks appear on the lemons; they'll be done when the hens are done. Transfer the grilled lemons to a serving platter and set aside.

Transfer the birds to a cutting board and let rest for 5 minutes. Use a chef's knife to cut each bird in half, down the middle. Place the hens on the serving platter. Serve immediately and encourage everyone to squeeze the grilled lemons on the birds.

# ROASTED HALIBUT WITH PEPERONATA

*Peperonata* is a simple rustic stew of peppers, onions, and tomatoes. Roasted potatoes make the stew a little heartier and more soul-satisfying and adds a different texture to the soft vegetables. This *peperonata* is also wonderful with roasted pork or served as a bruschetta topping.

*Pair with*
A DRY, FULL
WHITE WINE

Pick a wine with some good acidity. We like Emidio Pepe Trebbiano d'Abruzzo.

**SERVES 4**

### PEPERONATA

1½ pounds Yukon
  Gold potatoes,
  medium dice

¼ cup extra-
  virgin olive oil

1½ teaspoons
  kosher salt

Freshly cracked
  black pepper

1 white onion,
  small dice

5 garlic cloves, minced

¼ teaspoon red
  chili flakes, plus
  more to taste

2 red bell peppers,
  stems and seeds
  removed, small dice

1 yellow bell pepper,
  stems and seeds
  removed, small dice

1 bay leaf

½ cup dry white wine
  (such as Pinot Grigio)

1 (14- to 14.5-ounce)
  can chopped
  tomatoes, with juice

6 fresh basil leaves,
  torn into small pieces

1 tablespoon finely
  chopped flat-
  leaf parsley

### FISH

2 tablespoons extra-
  virgin olive oil

4 (4- to 6-ounce)
  halibut or cod fillets

Kosher salt and
  freshly cracked
  black pepper

4 lemon wedges

To make the *peperonata*, preheat the oven to 350°F. Toss the potatoes with 2 tablespoons of the olive oil. Season generously with ½ teaspoon of the salt and a few turns of the pepper. Spread the potatoes on a baking sheet and roast in the oven until tender, 30 to 35 minutes.

Meanwhile, heat a large sauté pan over medium-high heat with the remaining 2 tablespoons olive oil. When the oil is hot, add the onion, garlic, chili flakes, and ½ teaspoon of the salt. Sauté until the onion is soft, 5 to 10 minutes. Add the peppers and bay leaf. Continue sautéing until the peppers are soft, 10 minutes more.

# ROASTED HALIBUT WITH PEPERONATA
**CONTINUED**

Add the wine and cook until the pan is dry, 4 to 5 minutes. Add the tomatoes and the roasted potatoes. Add the remaining ½ teaspoon salt. Simmer until the liquid is reduced by half, 5 to 8 minutes. The *peperonata* can be made ahead to this point and stored in an airtight container in the refrigerator for a day or two; before continuing, heat the *peperonata* until hot.

Add the basil and parsley to the *peperonata*. Taste and adjust the seasoning; feel free to add more chili flakes to make the mixture slightly spicy. Keep warm while cooking the fish.

To make the fish, decrease the oven temperature (or preheat) to 300°F. Heat the olive oil in a large ovenproof sauté pan over medium-high heat. Season the fish fillets generously with salt and pepper. Gently place the fish fillets in the hot sauté pan. Sear the fish, without touching, until golden brown, 3 to 5 minutes. Using a fish spatula, gently turn the fish over. Immediately place the sauté pan with the fish in the oven. Cook in the oven until a thin metal skewer or metal cake tester slides easily in and out of the fish and the skewer feels warm against your lip, 3 to 5 minutes for halibut or a few minutes longer for cod.

Serve each fish fillet with the warm *peperonata*. Garnish each with a lemon wedge to squeeze over the fish.

# ARCTIC CHAR WITH LENTILS AND FRISÉE

My chef de cuisine at L'Apicio, Kaytlin Brakefield, deserves the credit for this dish. The lentils are served two ways: pureed and pickled in a dressing. Katherine tried to convince me that the pureed lentils were unnecessary—then she tried the sauce-like puree and realized that it brought the dish together. She also managed to eat all of the leftover puree with a spoon.

*Pair with*
A LIGHT
RED WINE

Choose a red with bright acidity. We like: Hirsch Vineyards "Bohan Dillon" Pinot Noir.

**SERVES 4**

### COOKED LENTILS

3 cups water

⅔ cup green lentils

3 garlic cloves

1 sprig fresh thyme

1 bay leaf

¼ teaspoon kosher salt

### LENTIL PUREE

¾ cup cooked green lentils

1 tablespoon extra-virgin olive oil

1 tablespoon water

2 teaspoons red wine vinegar

¼ teaspoon kosher salt, plus more as needed

### LENTIL VINAIGRETTE

¼ cup cooked green lentils

2 tablespoons extra-virgin olive oil

2 tablespoons red wine vinegar

1 tablespoon finely diced shallot

1 tablespoon finely diced carrot

1 tablespoon finely diced celery

Kosher salt and freshly cracked black pepper

### FISH

2 heads of frisée, bottoms and wilted leaves removed

1 tablespoon chopped fresh chives

4 (5-ounce) skin-on Arctic char or salmon fillets, at room temperature

Kosher salt and freshly cracked black pepper

2 tablespoons extra-virgin olive oil

High-quality extra-virgin olive oil, for drizzling

To cook the lentils, place the water, lentils, garlic, thyme, bay leaf, and salt in a medium (3-quart) saucepan. Bring the contents of the pan to a boil over high heat. Cover the pan and decrease the heat to low. Simmer the covered lentils until they are tender, 25 to 30 minutes. Drain the lentils through a fine-mesh strainer. Place in a small bowl. Discard the thyme, garlic, and bay leaf.

To make the lentil puree, place the ¾ cup cooked lentils in a small food processor. Add the oil, water, vinegar, and the ¼ teaspoon salt and process until smooth. The pureed lentils should resemble the consistency of hummus. If the mixture is too thick, add a small amount of water to loosen. Taste the lentil puree and add more salt if necessary. Place the puree in a small bowl and cover with plastic wrap. Let the puree sit in a warm location, such as near or above the oven or stove, until ready to serve.

To make the lentil vinaigrette, stir the ¼ cup cooked lentils with the olive oil, vinegar, shallot, carrot, and celery in a small bowl. Season the vinaigrette generously with the salt and freshly cracked pepper. The vinaigrette can be made 2 to 3 days ahead; keep refrigerated in an airtight container.

To make the fish, first separate the frisée leaves and place in a medium bowl with the chives. Set aside while cooking the fish.

Heat a large sauté pan over medium-high heat. Generously season both sides of the fillets with salt and pepper. Add the olive oil to the hot sauté pan. Add the fish fillets, skin side down, to the hot pan. Cook the fish undisturbed for 3 to 4 minutes, until the skin is golden and crispy. Using a metal spatula, gently flip the fish fillets to the other side. Turn off the heat. Let the fish fillets sit in the pan for 30 seconds to 2 minutes, until they are properly cooked. To test if the fish is ready, insert a metal skewer or metal cake tester into the center of the fish. The skewer should slide easily into the fish. Let the skewer sit in the middle of the fish for a few seconds. Remove the skewer and place it against your lip. It should feel slightly warm. When the fish is ready, remove the fish from the hot pan and set aside.

Meanwhile, place the lentil vinaigrette in a small sauté or saucepan over medium heat. Heat the vinaigrette until it is warm to the touch, not boiling. Pour the warm vinaigrette over the frisée and chives. Toss together. Taste and adjust the seasoning as needed.

Spread a dollop (2 to 3 tablespoons) of lentil puree on each serving plate. Place 1 fish fillet in the center of the puree on each plate. Distribute the frisée salad with warm lentil vinaigrette among the plates. Drizzle each fillet with high-quality extra-virgin olive oil. Serve immediately.

# BRANZINO AL CARTOCCIO

The name of this dish literally means "fish cooked in a paper bag." In reality, a packet made of parchment paper is stuffed with vegetables and a fish fillet, then sealed and placed in a hot oven. Inside the packet, magic occurs. The fish gently steams and absorbs some of the flavor of the vegetables, while the juices from the fish and vegetables combine to create a delicate sauce. When the packet is opened, a delicious aroma fills the air. Not only is this dish incredibly healthy, it is also very easy to prepare; you can make the packets several hours ahead of time and put them in the oven just before you're ready to serve. You can also have fun with the ingredients—this dish works with almost any thin filleted fish (bream, snapper, black bass) and vegetables (try thinly sliced zucchini in the summer, fennel and radicchio in the winter). Instead of the fregola pasta, you can use another cooked whole grain such as farro. Mix and match; you will be pleased with the results every time.

*Pair with*
A FRESH MINERAL WHITE WINE

For this fish dish, choose a coastal, slightly salty wine. We like: Sam Lorenzo Verdicchio, from Italy's Marche region.

## SERVES 4

4 ounces fregola pasta or Israeli couscous

½ teaspoon kosher salt, plus more for cooking grains

3½ tablespoons extra-virgin olive oil

1⅓ cups halved grape or cherry tomatoes

3 tablespoons thinly sliced scallion

2 tablespoons freshly squeezed lemon juice

1½ tablespoons minced fresh hot chili (red finger or red jalapeño)

7 Alfonso or kalamata olives, pitted and roughly chopped

1½ teaspoons finely grated lemon zest

4 (3- to 3½-ounce) branzino fillets

Freshly cracked black pepper

4 sprigs thyme

4 lemon wedges

To cook the fregola, bring a large pot of water to a boil. Season generously with salt. Taste the water and make sure that it tastes salty. Boil the fregola, stirring occasionally, until al dente, 8 to 10 minutes, depending on the size of the fregola. Drain thoroughly.

Place the cooked fregola in a medium bowl and toss with 1½ tablespoons of the olive oil. Add the tomatoes, scallion, lemon juice, chili, olives, lemon zest, and the ½ teaspoon salt. Toss together and set aside.

# BRANZINO AL CARTOCCIO
**CONTINUED**

Preheat the oven to 400°F. Season the fish fillets generously on both sides with salt and pepper. Arrange 4 pieces of parchment paper, each 12 inches by 17 inches, on a work surface. Fold each piece of parchment paper in half so that the sheets are approximately 12 inches by 8½ inches. Open the parchment paper like a book and spoon one-quarter of the fregola salad onto one-half of each piece of parchment paper. Lay the fish fillets on top of the fregola, skin side up. Drizzle 1½ teaspoons of olive oil over each piece of fish. Place one thyme sprig atop each fillet. Fold the parchment paper over the fish fillets to close the book. Starting at the short side of each book, roll or crimp the edges of the parchment to create a tightly sealed packet (it will look like a half-moon when you're done). Place 2 fish packets on each of 2 baking sheets, leaving a little space between the packets.

Bake the fish packets for 15 minutes. Serve each packet, parchment paper and all, on a plate with a wedge of lemon. Let guests open their own packets by puncturing the top half of the parchment paper with a knife and fork, and drizzling the fish with freshly squeezed lemon juice.

# STRIPED BASS WITH BRAISED FENNEL AND BASS DRESSING

Shortly after dell'anima opened, we came up with a preserved lemon dressing to serve with striped bass. It is a room-temperature lemon salsa that is also delicious with Arctic char, tuna salad, raw fish, chicken . . . pretty much anything. But since it originally was served with bass, this condiment will forever be known in our kitchen as "bass dressing." Striped bass is a delicious, meaty white fish. If it's unavailable in your area, substitute a white fish of your choice, such as black bass, snapper, halibut, or cobia.

*Pair with*
A WHITE WINE WITH GOOD ACIDITY

The wine should have plenty of personality. We like: De Conciliis "Donnaluna" Fiano.

## SERVES 4

### BRAISED FENNEL

2 large fennel bulbs

4 cups water

2 cups dry white wine (such as Pinot Grigio)

10 whole black peppercorns

10 sprigs fresh thyme

6 garlic cloves

Zest of 2 lemons, peeled with a vegetable peeler

½ teaspoon kosher salt

### BASS DRESSING

1 preserved lemon, soaked overnight in fresh water (see Note)

3 tablespoons juice from jar of hot pickled peppers (or 3 tablespoons white vinegar and ⅛ teaspoon chili oil)

2 tablespoons extra-virgin olive oil

2 tablespoons minced shallot

1 tablespoon finely grated fresh lemon zest

### FISH

4 (4-ounce) striped bass fillets, skin on

4 to 5 tablespoons extra-virgin olive oil

1½ tablespoons freshly squeezed lemon juice

1½ tablespoons finely chopped fresh flat-leaf parsley

Kosher salt and freshly cracked black pepper

# STRIPED BASS WITH BRAISED FENNEL AND BASS DRESSING
## CONTINUED

To prepare the fennel, trim the top and bottom of each fennel bulb. Slice each bulb in half lengthwise. Then slice each half lengthwise from the center outward into 6 wedges. Place the fennel wedges in a medium (3-quart) saucepan. Add the water, wine, peppercorns, thyme, garlic, lemon zest, and salt to the saucepan. Place over high heat and bring to a boil. Decrease the heat to low. Place a round piece of parchment paper over the fennel to keep the fennel submerged in the braising liquid. Keeping the liquid at just under a simmer on low heat, braise the fennel, uncovered, until the wedges are tender and can be easily pierced with a metal skewer or fork, but still retain their shape and structure, about 15 minutes. Remove from the heat, discard the parchment paper, and let the fennel cool in the braising liquid for at least 20 minutes. The fennel can be made ahead and stored, submerged in the poaching liquid, in an airtight container in the refrigerator for 2 to 3 days. If cooking immediately, drain the poaching liquid, discard the aromatics, and set aside the fennel to be sautéed later.

While the fennel is braising, make the bass dressing. Rinse the soaked preserved lemon thoroughly in cold water. Slice the lemon lengthwise into 4 pieces. Use a spoon or paring knife to remove the pith area. Finely dice the preserved lemon zest and place in a small bowl. Add the 3 tablespoons pickling juice, the olive oil, shallot, and fresh lemon zest. Stir to combine. The dressing can be made a week in advance and stored in an airtight covered container in the refrigerator.

To prepare the fish, place the fish on a plate or board and let it come to room temperature.

Meanwhile, heat a large sauté pan over high heat with 1 tablespoon of the oil. Scatter half of the braised fennel over the hot pan. Sauté the fennel until the wedges are slightly golden brown, about 5 minutes. Place the sautéed fennel in a large bowl. Repeat with another 1 tablespoon of oil and the remaining fennel. Add the bass dressing, lemon juice, and parsley to the fennel. Set aside while cooking the fish.

Heat a large skillet or sauté pan over high heat. Season the fish generously on both sides with salt and pepper. Add 2 to 3 tablespoons of olive oil to the hot pan. Gently place the fish in the pan, skin side down. Cook the fish undisturbed for 3 to 5 minutes, until the skin is crispy and golden brown. Using a metal spatula, gently flip the fish fillets over. Turn off the heat. Let the fish fillets sit in the pan until they are properly cooked, 30 seconds to 2 minutes, depending on the thickness of the fish. To test if the fish is ready, insert a metal skewer or metal cake tester into the center of the fish. The skewer should slide easily into the fish. Let the skewer sit in the middle of the fish for a few seconds. Remove the skewer and place it against your lip. It should feel slightly warm. When the fish is ready, transfer to a serving platter or to individual serving plates. Serve the fish immediately with the fennel.

**NOTE:** Preserved lemons add intensely lemony, slightly exotic flavor to a dish. They can be purchased at specialty food stores.

# WHOLE ROASTED TURBOT WITH SUMMER SUCCOTASH

Serving a whole fish, such as turbot, is unbelievably impressive to guests. The secret that your guests don't know is that it is surprisingly easy to make. Simply roast the fish, peel off the skin, and gently remove the fish fillets. While this process is straightforward, you'll need to take a deep breath, have patience, and do not get discouraged if your kitchen gets a little messy. Don't throw out the bones—store them in the freezer to make a spectacular fish stock on another day.

*Pair with*
A RICH, FULL
WHITE WINE

We like: Grenache Blanc from Donkey & Goat, a California winery using natural, artisanal techniques.

## SERVES 4

3 tablespoons extra-virgin olive oil

1 (2½-pound) turbot, gills removed, at room temperature

Maldon sea salt flakes

2 to 3 tablespoons high-quality extra-virgin olive oil, for drizzling

Freshly squeezed juice of half of a lemon

Summer Succotash (recipe follows)

Preheat the oven to 400°F. Turn a baking sheet upside down (this will make it easier to remove the fish later). Drizzle the baking sheet with 1½ tablespoons of the olive oil. Place the turbot on the baking sheet with the dark side facing up. Using the tip of a sharp paring knife, gently trace the outline between the fins and the fish; you want to just detach the skin without cutting through the flesh. Leave the skin in place. Drizzle the remaining 1½ tablespoons olive oil over the fish. Place the baking sheet with the fish in the oven and bake for 20 to 25 minutes, until properly cooked. To test if the fish is done, place a thermometer in the thickest part of the fish (by the neck, near the head). The desired temperature is 140°F. Or use a metal skewer in the same area. The skewer should slide easily into the fish. Let the skewer sit in the middle of the fish for a few seconds. Remove the skewer and place it against your lip. It should feel slightly warm.

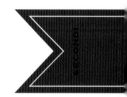

When the fish is cooked, be sure to show off the whole fish to your family or guests. To serve the fish, use a paring knife to gently remove the dark skin from the flesh. Once a small amount of skin is removed, it is easy to peel off the whole piece of skin with your hands. Discard the dark skin. Using a fish spatula or an offset spatula, gently remove the fish fillets, starting from the center of the backbone and moving outward. Place the fish fillets on serving plates or a platter. Gently peel off and discard the backbone; it should remove easily. Once again, use a fish spatula or offset spatula to remove the bottom fish fillets from the bottom layer of skin. Place these thinner fish fillets on the serving plates or platter. Discard the fish scraps.

Season the fish fillets with Maldon sea salt flakes and drizzle with high-quality extra-virgin olive oil and freshly squeezed lemon juice. Serve with the warm succotash.

# WHOLE ROASTED TURBOT WITH SUMMER SUCCOTASH
**CONTINUED**

## SUMMER SUCCOTASH

I hate lima beans. They taste awful. So even though traditional succotash calls for lima beans and corn, I replace the lima beans with green beans. I also see succotash as an excuse to include whatever ingredients are available at the market: squash, tomatoes, onions. The inclusion of basil and lemon makes the dish taste a little floral. It is a delicate flavor that works well with the turbot. The green beans and corn kernels can be prepared in advance; complete the dish while the fish is in the oven.

**SERVES 4**

Kosher salt

4 ounces green
  beans, trimmed

2 ears of fresh white
  or yellow corn

2 tablespoons extra-
  virgin olive oil

¾ cup small dice
  Spanish onion

1½ teaspoons fresh
  thyme leaves

1¼ cups small dice
  yellow squash
  and/or zucchini

Small pinch of red
  chili flakes

¾ cup cherry
  tomatoes, halved

1½ teaspoons finely
  grated lemon zest

4 fresh basil
  leaves, torn

Bring a large pot of water to a boil. Season the water generously with salt until it tastes very salty, like the sea. Blanch the green beans in the boiling water until they are tender and soft, 5 to 6 minutes. Remove the green beans from the boiling water and place on a baking sheet or plate in the refrigerator. After 10 to 15 minutes, when cool enough to touch, slice the green beans diagonally into ½-inch lengths. Set aside.

Using a chef's knife, slice the kernels off the corncobs and place in a small bowl. Working over the bowl, use the back of the chef's knife to scrape the corn juice from each cob. The green beans and corn can be prepared about 2 hours in advance and stored in the refrigerator until ready to use; let come to room temperature before using.

Place a large sauté pan over high heat. Add the olive oil, onion, thyme, and a generous pinch of salt. Sauté the onion, stirring frequently, until it starts to turn a golden color, about 5 minutes. Add the corn with juice, the squash, red chili flakes, and another generous pinch of salt. Sauté for 5 minutes. Add the cherry tomatoes and blanched green beans and sauté for another 5 minutes. Turn off the heat. Add the lemon zest and basil; stir to combine. Taste and adjust the seasoning as needed. Let the succotash remain in the hot pan until the main course is ready.

# NEW YORK STRIP STEAKS WITH SALSA VERDE POTATOES

You can't go wrong with meat and potatoes. This version features my favorite steak: New York strip. There is very little gristle on this cut of meat and when properly marbleized, it melts in your mouth. The potatoes are tossed in a pesto-like green sauce and served like a warm potato salad.

*Pair with*
SANGIOVESE

This is my favorite grape for steak because it has both acidity and tannin. We like: Fontodi Chianti Classico—or spring for the outstanding Flaccianello.

## SERVES 4

- 2 pounds baby Yukon gold potatoes or fingerling potatoes
- 2 tablespoons extra-virgin olive oil
- 2 teaspoons kosher salt, plus more for seasoning

- Freshly cracked black pepper
- Leaves from 3 sprigs of fresh rosemary (about ¼ cup rosemary leaves)
- 2 (13 to 14-ounce) New York strip steaks, each about 1½ inches thick

- Salsa Verde (recipe follows)
- High-quality extra-virgin olive oil, for drizzling
- Maldon sea salt flakes (optional)

Preheat the oven to 400°F. In a large bowl, toss together the potatoes, 1 tablespoon of the olive oil, the salt, about 20 turns of pepper, and the rosemary leaves. Spread the potatoes onto a baking sheet. Roast until the potatoes are tender when pierced with a fork, 45 minutes to 1 hour. Remove from the oven and let cool. Increase the oven temperature to 450°F.

When cool enough to touch, smash each potato with the palm of your hand so that it flattens into a ½-inch-thick disk. If the potatoes appear messy, do not worry. The messier they look, the better they will taste slathered in the salsa verde and meat juice. The potatoes can be cooked in advance and stored in the refrigerator, but make sure they are at room temperature when you are ready to cook the steak.

While the potatoes are cooking, let the steaks rest at room temperature for 30 minutes to 1 hour before cooking.

Generously season the steaks with salt and pepper on all sides. Do not be shy with the seasoning. The more salt, the better.

Place a large cast-iron skillet over high heat (or place in the oven for a few minutes and return to the stovetop over high heat). When hot, add the remaining 1 tablespoon oil. Working with 1 steak at a time, use tongs to hold the steak on its side and place the cap of fat on the skillet. Once the fat cap has rendered (1 to 2 minutes), remove the steak completely and repeat with the other steak. Then gently add both steaks to the pan, laying them flat on one side. Cook undisturbed for 3 to 4 minutes. Gently turn the steaks over and cook for another 3 to 4 minutes. Remove the steaks from the skillet (do not wipe out the skillet) and let rest. Depending on the heat of your stove and the thickness of the steaks, a total cooking time of 7 to 8 minutes should yield a medium temperature, with the steaks pink all the way through (as all steaks should be served).

After removing the steaks, add the potatoes to the skillet. Immediately place the skillet in the hot oven. After 3 minutes, toss the potatoes in the skillet and return to the oven for another 3 minutes, or until slightly browned and hot. Transfer the potatoes to a large bowl with ¼ cup of the salsa verde. Toss together. Taste and adjust the seasoning as needed. Arrange the potatoes on a serving platter.

With a sharp knife, thinly slice the steaks against the grain. Place the slices of steak on the potatoes. Lightly drizzle the steak with high-quality extra-virgin olive oil. Serve with Maldon, if desired, and the remaining salsa verde.

# SALSA VERDE

Almost every culture has its own interpretation of salsa verde, a cold sauce consisting of pureed herbs, vinegar, and oil. I like to spice it up with hot pickled pepper and to enhance the acidity with both pickling juice and lemon. I prefer to chop all of the ingredients by hand. With this technique, I feel that the shallots retain more structure and the parsley does not bruise. But if you are in a crunch for time, roughly chop all of the ingredients and pulse in a food processor or blender. The sauce is best served the day that it is made; it will discolor over time. Salsa verde is excellent served with roasted fish, chicken, or pork ribs.

## MAKES 1 CUP

¼ cup minced shallots

1 tablespoon finely chopped hot pickled pepper (B&G brand preferred), stems and seeds removed

¼ cup pickling liquid from jar of B&G hot pickled peppers

1½ cloves garlic, germ removed, finely grated on a Microplane

1 tablespoon chopped capers

½ cup chopped fresh flat-leaf parsley

Freshly grated zest of 1 lemon (about 1½ teaspoons)

⅛ teaspoon kosher salt

¼ cup extra-virgin olive oil

In a medium bowl, stir together the shallots, pickled pepper, pickling liquid, garlic, capers, parsley, lemon zest, salt, and oil. Keep refrigerated until ready to serve. The salsa is best served the day you make it.

# VEAL MILANESE WITH ARUGULA AND PARMESAN

The traditional veal Milanese recipe consists of pounded veal drenched in eggs, coated with breadcrumbs and Parmesan, and fried in butter. I prefer to cook the meat the way they make a chicken-fried steak at a Texas diner: dipping the meat in a seasoned flour mixture, then in egg, and then again in the flour mixture. The veal can be replaced with chicken, pork, or beef. Be sure to eat each bite with a generous amount of lemony arugula, which balances the delicious fat of the fried cutlet.

*Pair with*
SPARKLING WINE

Milan is the capital of Lombardia, which produces Italy's finest sparkling wines—and bubbles are best with food. We like: Lambrusco from Lini910, Luciano Saetti, or Camillo Donati.

**SERVES 4**

- 12 ounces veal top round
- ½ teaspoon kosher salt, plus more for seasoning
- ½ teaspoon freshly cracked black pepper, plus more for seasoning
- 2 cups unbleached all-purpose flour
- ½ teaspoon dried thyme
- ½ teaspoon dried rosemary
- ½ teaspoon dried sage
- ½ teaspoon dried oregano
- 2 large eggs
- 1 cup milk
- Olive oil or vegetable oil, for frying
- 4 large handfuls of baby arugula
- Freshly squeezed juice of 1 lemon
- 2 tablespoons extra-virgin olive oil
- ⅓ cup grated Parmesan cheese
- 4 lemon wedges

Preheat the oven to 300°F. Place a baking sheet with a rack in the oven.

Slice the veal into 4 equal pieces. Using the flat side of a meat mallet or skillet, pound each piece of veal between wax paper or parchment paper until it is just under ¼ inch thick. Season each piece of veal on both sides with salt and pepper.

In a medium bowl, combine the flour, thyme, rosemary, sage, oregano, the ½ teaspoon salt, and the ½ teaspoon pepper. In another medium bowl, whisk together the eggs and milk. Working with 1 piece of veal at a time, place the veal in the flour mixture to coat both sides. Shake off the excess flour. Place the floured veal in the egg mixture, coating completely. Then return the veal to the flour mixture. Coat both sides and shake off the excess flour. Set the veal aside on a large plate. Repeat this process with the remaining 3 pieces of veal.

Place a large skillet over medium-high heat. Add a thin layer of olive oil or vegetable oil to coat the bottom of the pan. When the oil is hot, gently place 1 piece of veal in the pan. Cook undisturbed until the veal is golden brown on the bottom, 2 to 3 minutes. Carefully turn the veal to cook the other side for an additional 2 to 3 minutes. Remove the veal from the pan and place the veal on the rack in the oven. Repeat this process 1 piece of veal at a time. If at any point the contents of the pan start to blacken or burn, discard the oil, wash the pan, and start the process again.

Place the arugula in a large bowl. Drizzle with the lemon juice and extra-virgin olive oil. Season the arugula with salt and pepper. Sprinkle the Parmesan on the greens. Toss together. Taste and adjust the seasoning as needed. Distribute the dressed arugula among the serving plates. Place the veal next to the greens. Garnish with lemon wedges to squeeze over the veal. Serve immediately.

# BRAISED SHORT RIBS WITH POLENTA

This is a great dish for entertaining, because you can braise the ribs the day before, let them sit in the sauce overnight, then simply reheat to serve. The flavors become even richer over time. The key to any braise is to go slow and low—it is impossible to rush the braising process, but the results are well worth the wait. Note that there will be extra sauce after serving the ribs, which you can toss with pasta or meatballs, or pour over meat loaf. Consider it a killer Sunday gravy.

*Pair with*
A FULL, DRY
RED WINE

Aglianico or Sagrantino would work well with the ribs. We like: Cantine Lonardo for Aglianico, Paolo Bea for Sagrantino.

## SERVES 4

4 (12-ounce) portions beef short ribs, with bones

1 teaspoon kosher salt, plus more for seasoning

Freshly cracked black pepper

¼ cup extra-virgin olive oil

2½ cups medium dice Spanish onions

¾ cup medium dice carrots

½ cup medium dice celery

1 tablespoon tomato paste

2 cups dry red wine (such as Cabernet)

1 (28-ounce) can whole or chopped Italian tomatoes, with juice

1 bay leaf

Polenta (page 95), for serving

Freshly grated Parmesan cheese, for garnish (optional)

To make the short ribs, let the ribs sit at room temperature for 30 minutes. Season the ribs generously on all sides with a large amount of salt and pepper.

In a large cast-iron skillet, heat 2 tablespoons of the olive oil over medium-high heat. When the oil is hot, gently place the short ribs in the skillet. Do not touch the short ribs. Let them caramelize. When the short ribs have a dark brown color on the bottom (about 4 minutes), gently turn them to sear another side. Continue this process until all of the sides of the short ribs are dark brown, about 10 minutes total. Remove the ribs from the skillet and set aside.

Place the remaining 2 tablespoons olive oil, the onions, carrots, celery, and ½ teaspoon of the salt in a large ovenproof Dutch oven. Sauté the vegetables over medium-high heat until the vegetables are soft and begin to caramelize, 5 to 8 minutes. Add the tomato paste. Cook, stirring constantly, for 2 minutes, scraping the bottom of the Dutch oven. Add the wine to the Dutch oven, and continue cooking until the liquid is reduced by half, about 10 minutes.

# BRAISED SHORT RIBS WITH POLENTA
## CONTINUED

Preheat the oven to 300°F. Add the tomatoes, bay leaf, and ½ teaspoon of the salt to the Dutch oven. Bring to a simmer. Place the short ribs in the Dutch oven. Cover tightly and place in the preheated oven. After 30 minutes, gently turn the ribs over. Return to the oven for another 30 minutes; gently turn the ribs again. Continue cooking the short ribs, checking them periodically, until a thin metal skewer slides easily in and out of the ribs (there should be no tension at all) and the meat comes easily off the bone, 1½ to 2 hours total. Be sure to test each rib in multiple areas. Depending on the size of the ribs, some will cook more quickly than others. As soon as they are tender, remove them from the oven; overcooked short ribs will be dry and unappealing.

Meanwhile, make the polenta. When the ribs are done, remove from the oven and decrease the oven temperature to 200°F. Keep the polenta in the 200°F oven, covered, until ready to serve.

Remove the bay leaf from the rib sauce and discard. Gently remove the short ribs from the sauce. Spoon off and discard any excess fat. Puree the sauce in a food processor or blender. Taste and adjust the seasoning as needed. Return the sauce to the Dutch oven. Remove and discard the short rib bones. Trim the fat and extra cartilage from the short ribs. Return the ribs to the Dutch oven with the sauce. Hold in a warm 200°F oven until ready to serve, up to 1½ hours.

Before serving, warm the serving bowls. Whisk the polenta; if it appears to be too thick, thin it out with a little water. Otherwise, ladle a ½ cup portion of polenta into each warm serving bowl. Place 1 portion braised short ribs in each dish. Ladle a generous amount of sauce over the short ribs. Garnish with grated Parmesan cheese, if desired.

# BRAISED LAMB SHANKS WITH CRANBERRY BEANS, BUTTERNUT SQUASH, AND TOMATOES

This is the perfect dish for colder weather, with a variety of fall flavors that work really well together. There are several components, but the cranberry bean mixture can be prepared while the lamb shanks braise. If you would rather not serve the lamb shanks whole (one shank per person is a super-generous portion), pick the meat off of the bone, chop it, and turn the dish into a stew or pasta sauce (it's great with rigatoni), or serve it on top of polenta.

*Pair with*
A BIG, JUICY
RED WINE

We like: Zinfandel from Turley Wine Cellars.

## SERVES 4

### BRAISED LAMB

4 (1½-pound) bone-in lamb shanks

1 teaspoon kosher salt, plus more for seasoning

Freshly cracked black pepper

6 tablespoons extra-virgin olive oil

4 cups medium dice yellow onions

3 tablespoons finely chopped garlic

Pinch of red chili flakes

1 cup dry white wine (such as Pinot Grigio)

2 cups canned diced tomatoes, with juice

2 sprigs fresh rosemary, tied together with butcher's twine

1 bay leaf

### CRANBERRY BEANS

2 tablespoons extra-virgin olive oil

4 ounces lamb sausage, casings removed (see Note)

1½ cups small dice yellow onions

2 tablespoons finely chopped garlic

1 tablespoon fresh oregano leaves

Kosher salt

Red chili flakes

½ cup dry white wine (such as Pinot Grigio)

2 cups canned diced tomatoes, with juice

1½ cups medium dice butternut squash

3 cups cooked cranberry beans (recipe follows)

High-quality extra-virgin olive oil, for drizzling

# BRAISED LAMB SHANKS
**CONTINUED**

To prepare the lamb shanks, preheat the oven to 300°F. Remove any excess fat and silver skin. Heat a large sauté pan or cast-iron skillet over high heat. Season the lamb shanks generously with salt and pepper. Place 2 tablespoons of the oil in the hot pan. Using tongs, carefully add 2 of the lamb shanks to the hot pan. Sear the shanks undisturbed until the bottoms are golden brown and easily release from the hot pan, 2 to 3 minutes. Turn the shanks to sear another side. Repeat until the lamb shanks are seared on all sides. Remove the shanks from the pan and set aside on a baking sheet or plate. Discard the oil from the pan. Repeat this process with 2 more tablespoons of the oil and the remaining lamb shanks.

To make the braising liquid, place a large ovenproof Dutch oven over high heat. Add the remaining 2 tablespoons olive oil, the onions, garlic, the 1 teaspoon salt, and the chili flakes. Sauté the onion mixture, stirring frequently, until the onions are soft and start to take on a golden color, about 5 minutes. Add the wine and cook until most of the wine has evaporated, 3 to 4 minutes. Add the tomatoes, rosemary, and bay leaf. Bring the mixture to a boil.

Add the lamb shanks to the braising mixture. Cover the pan and place in the oven. Cook the shanks in the oven for 1½ to 2 hours, until the meat is tender and naturally releases itself from the bone. I like to use a couple of forks to separate a chunk of meat; if the meat separates easily, it is ready. If the meat seems to hold on with any sort of tension, continue braising the shanks and check again in another 15 to 20 minutes.

When done, remove the pan from the oven and discard the rosemary and bay leaf. Set aside 2½ cups of the braising liquid and vegetables.

While the lamb is braising, prepare the cranberry bean mixture. Place the olive oil in a medium (3-quart) saucepan over medium-high heat. Add the lamb sausage. Using a wooden spoon, break the sausage into smaller chunks. Cook until the sausage is golden brown, 3 to 5 minutes.

Add the onions, garlic, and oregano. Season the onion mixture generously with salt and a pinch of red chili flakes. Sauté, stirring frequently, until the onions are soft and begin to take on a slight golden color, 5 to 7 minutes. Add the wine to the pan. Cook until the wine has completely evaporated, about 3 minutes. Add the tomatoes and butternut squash and bring to a simmer. Taste the liquid to make sure it is properly seasoned. Add a pinch or two of salt if necessary. Cover the pan and turn the heat down to low. Let the mixture cook for 15 minutes. Add the cooked beans and the reserved 2½ cups of braising liquid and vegetables from the lamb shanks. Taste a piece of the butternut squash. It should be tender, but still retain its shape. If the squash is at all crunchy, continue simmering the mixture for another 5 to 10 minutes, until the squash is properly cooked. Taste and adjust the seasoning.

To serve, ladle a ½- to ¾-cup portion of the cranberry bean mixture into each warm serving bowl. Place a lamb shank, bone and all, in each bowl. Drizzle each shank with high-quality extra-virgin olive oil.

**NOTE:** I was inspired to use lamb sausage when I saw it at our local butcher, Ottomanelli's, on Bleecker Street. It adds great depth of flavor to the cranberry bean mixture, but if it is unavailable, feel free to substitute merguez or pork sausage. Or season some ground lamb with dried herbs (rosemary, thyme, oregano), salt, and pepper. But by no means is the sausage mandatory—this dish is delicious without it, too.

## CRANBERRY BEANS

When cranberry beans, or borlotti beans, are cooked, they look similar to pinto beans, but the flavor is much more elegant and less pronounced. Cranberry beans are one of my favorite ingredients. They are wonderful tossed in pasta, or pureed into a creamy, sexy soup or sauce. If you don't have the time to soak and cook dried beans, jarred or canned borlotti beans are usually sold at Italian specialty stores.

### MAKES ENOUGH FOR 4 SERVINGS

4 cups water

1 cup dried cranberry beans, soaked overnight

¼ cup extra-virgin olive oil

2 celery stalks

1 carrot

¼ Spanish onion

1 bay leaf

1 teaspoon kosher salt

Place the water, cranberry beans, olive oil, celery, carrot, onion, and bay leaf in a medium (3-quart) saucepan. Bring to a boil over high heat. Decrease the heat to low and keep the beans just under a simmer until the beans are soft and tender, but still retain their shape, 1 to 1½ hours. Toward the end of the cooking time, add the salt. When the beans are done, remove from the heat and let the beans cool in the cooking liquid. Discard the celery, carrot, onion, and bay leaf. Drain the cooking liquid from the beans when ready to use. The beans can be prepared ahead of time and stored in their cooking liquid in an airtight container for 4 to 5 days in the refrigerator or 2 to 3 weeks in the freezer.

# LEG OF LAMB WITH WILTED SPINACH AND GARLIC CONFIT

Rubbed with a simple herb-garlic mixture and roasted to the proper temperature, this leg of lamb makes a great crowd-pleasing dish. The most daunting part about leg of lamb is removing the bone and butterflying the meat—so let your butcher do this for you. You might need to order this cut of meat in advance.

*Pair with*
AN EARTHY, DRY RED WINE

You want herbal notes and an earthiness that pairs well with lamb and greens. We like: A Chinon from Olga Raffault made from Cabernet Franc grapes.

## SERVES 4 TO 6

### LAMB RUB

2½ to 3 pounds boneless leg of lamb (about ½ of 1 large leg), butterflied

Kosher salt and freshly cracked black pepper

3 tablespoons extra-virgin olive oil

1 tablespoon chopped garlic

1½ teaspoons roughly chopped fresh rosemary leaves

1½ teaspoons fresh oregano leaves

1½ teaspoons fresh thyme leaves

½ teaspoon red chili flakes

### WILTED SPINACH AND GARLIC CONFIT

1 head of garlic (about 20 cloves), cloves separated and peeled

1¼ cups extra-virgin olive oil

Kosher salt

½ cup sliced kalamata or Alfonso olives, pits removed

1 tablespoon fresh oregano leaves

Red chili flakes

1 pound fresh spinach, excess stems removed

### SERVING

High-quality extra-virgin olive oil, for drizzling

Maldon sea salt flakes (optional)

To prepare the lamb, preheat the oven to 300°F. Lay the meat flat on a surface with the inside of the lamb facing upward. Trim any excess fat or sinew. Season the meat generously with salt and pepper.

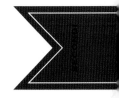

# LEG OF LAMB WITH WILTED SPINACH AND GARLIC CONFIT
**CONTINUED**

Place 1 tablespoon of the olive oil, the garlic, rosemary, oregano, thyme, and chili flakes in a mini food processor. Pulse until the mixture is a thick, pesto-like paste. Alternatively, you can use a mortar and pestle. Spread the herb mixture all over the interior of the lamb. Roll up the lamb lengthwise and use butcher's twine to tie the meat, first in the middle, then outward at 1-inch intervals. The lamb will look like a jelly roll. Season the exterior of the lamb with salt and pepper.

Heat a large cast-iron skillet or sauté pan over high heat. Add the remaining 2 tablespoons olive oil. Gently place the lamb in the hot pan. Cook undisturbed until the bottom of the lamb roast is golden brown and releases easily from the pan, about 5 minutes. Using tongs, rotate the lamb to cook another side. Repeat this process until the lamb is evenly browned on all sides. Remove the lamb from the hot pan and place on a rack in a roasting pan.

Roast the meat until the internal temperature registers 125°F, about 1 hour, depending on the size and shape of the lamb. Be sure to take the temperature after 30 to 35 minutes and check periodically after that; once the temperature of the meat reaches 100°F, it will increase rapidly thereafter. When the lamb reaches the proper temperature, transfer it to a baking sheet with a rack and let rest for 20 to 30 minutes at room temperature.

While the lamb is in the oven, prepare the garlic confit. Place the garlic cloves, olive oil, and a generous pinch of salt in a small (1-quart) saucepan. Cover the pan and place over low heat. Cook slowly until the garlic is soft, but still retains its shape, about 40 minutes. Remove from the heat. Drain and reserve the oil. Place the cooked garlic cloves on a cutting board and allow to cool for a few minutes. When cool enough to touch, use a paring knife to cut each garlic clove into 3 or 4 pieces.

While the lamb is resting at room temperature, prepare the spinach. Place 1 tablespoon of the garlic oil, half of the garlic, ¼ cup of the olives, 1½ teaspoons of the oregano leaves, a pinch of red chili flakes, and a pinch of salt in a large sauté pan. Set the pan over medium-high heat. Let the mixture cook until the ingredients start to sizzle and the garlic starts to turn a golden color, 3 to 4 minutes. Add half of the spinach and season generously with salt. Using tongs, gently turn the spinach in the hot garlic mixture and cook until the spinach is slightly wilted, 1 to 2 minutes. Transfer the contents of the pan to a large serving platter. Repeat this process with 1 tablespoon of garlic oil, the remaining half of the garlic, the remaining ¼ cup olives, the remaining 1½ teaspoons oregano, a pinch of red chili flakes, a pinch of salt, and the remaining half of the spinach. Transfer the spinach to the serving platter.

To serve the lamb, remove and discard the butcher's twine. Thinly slice the lamb into ¼-inch-thick slices. Lay the slices on top of the spinach on the platter. Drizzle the lamb with high-quality extra-virgin olive oil. Serve with Maldon sea salt flakes on the side.

# ROASTED PORK RACK WITH PLUMS AND CHORIZO

There are certain combinations of food that I go to over and over again. For example, pork works beautifully next to sweeter ingredients such as fruit. I also like to serve fresh pork with cured pork. Here is a combination of all of those flavors. The sweet and sour flavors of the plums balance out the smokiness of the chorizo and complement the caramelization of the fresh pork.

*Pair with*
A LIGHT BUT FLAVORFUL RED WINE

A red from northern Italy would be best here. We like: Ar.Pe.Pe. Valtellina Rosso Nebbiolo or a young Langhe Nebbiolo from Albino Rocca.

**SERVES 4 TO 6**

1 (2½-pound) bone-in pork rack with fat layer

Kosher salt and freshly cracked black pepper

¼ cup extra-virgin olive oil

3 ounces Spanish chorizo, small dice (see Note)

6 to 8 fresh basil leaves, torn into small pieces

8 to 10 plums, halved (quartered if large), pits removed

1 tablespoon acacia or clover honey

¼ cup chicken stock

High-quality extra-virgin olive oil, for drizzling

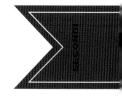

Preheat the oven to 350°F. Let the pork rack sit at room temperature for 30 to 45 minutes. Season the pork rack with salt and pepper. Make sure that the meat is completely covered with the seasoning.

Heat a large sauté pan over medium-high heat. Add 2 tablespoons of the olive oil. When the oil is hot, gently place the pork rack in the pan, fat side down. Do not touch the meat. When the meat is brown and caramelized (10 to 15 minutes), gently turn to caramelize another side (1 to 2 minutes on the other sides). Continue this process until the pork is seared and brown all over.

Place the pork on a rack in a roasting pan, making sure the fat is facing up. Roast until the internal temperature registers 125°F, 50 minutes to 1 hour. Remove the pork from the roasting pan and let rest on a rack with the fat facing up. Let the meat rest at room temperature for 30 minutes.

While the pork is resting, heat a large sauté pan over medium-high heat. Add the remaining 2 tablespoons olive oil and the chorizo to the pan. Sauté the chorizo until the fat is rendered and the chorizo is slightly crispy, 1 to 2 minutes.

# ROASTED PORK RACK WITH PLUMS AND CHORIZO
**CONTINUED**

Add the basil to the hot pan. It will instantly become aromatic. Take the sauté pan off the heat and carefully add the plums to the pan, cut side down. Return the sauté pan to the heat. Season generously with salt. Sauté until the plums are hot and slightly golden brown, 3 to 5 minutes. Drizzle the honey over the plums and stir. Add the chicken stock and reduce by half, about 2 minutes. Taste and adjust the seasoning as needed. Transfer the sautéed plums and chorizo to a serving platter.

To serve the pork, slice the pork rack into chops with 1 bone in each chop. Alternatively, cut the pork loin away from the bones and thinly slice the pork loin. Arrange the pork on the serving platter surrounded by the plums and chorizo. Drizzle the pork with high-quality extra-virgin olive oil.

**NOTE:** Spanish chorizo is a cured sausage that is heavily seasoned with smoked paprika. Don't confuse it with Mexican chorizo, which is a fresh sausage seasoned with chilies. The flavor and texture of the two chorizos are like night and day. While Mexican chorizo is delicious, the flavor is not appropriate here. If I can't find Spanish chorizo, I'll use soppressata, pancetta, or bacon instead.

# PORCINI-RUBBED VENISON WITH ROASTED MUSHROOMS AND WALNUTS

Hunting is a popular sport in my home state of Texas and game meats are featured on menus everywhere. Venison is my favorite—it's very lean and has a unique flavor that is more approachable than that of other game meats. But be careful: Venison cooks relatively quickly and if overcooked will become dry with a metallic taste, so be sure to use a meat thermometer and check the internal temperature frequently. When cooked properly, the flavor of venison complements the earthiness of the mushrooms and walnuts.

*Pair with*
A SAVORY, PEPPERY RED WINE

We like: A Teroldego from Foradori—the deep berry flavor goes well with venison.

**SERVES 4**

1 pound Denver roast of venison (see Note)

Kosher salt and freshly cracked black pepper

¼ cup porcini powder (or dried porcini mushrooms, pulverized in a food processor or spice grinder)

12 ounces assorted mushrooms (such as hen-of-the-woods, porcini, oyster, and/or shiitake), stems removed

6 tablespoons extra-virgin olive oil

5 tablespoons unsalted butter

⅓ cup walnut pieces

1 tablespoon chopped fresh oregano leaves

1 teaspoon finely chopped fresh rosemary leaves

½ cup dry white wine (such as Pinot Grigio)

2 cups chicken stock

2 cups mushroom or vegetable stock (or additional chicken stock)

1 teaspoon white vinegar

High-quality extra-virgin olive oil, for drizzling

Maldon sea salt flakes

To prepare the roast, trim off any silver skin. Generously season the roast with salt and pepper, then with the porcini powder. Every part of the roast should be generously coated in the powder. Set aside at room temperature until ready to cook.

Remove any fibrous ends of the mushrooms. Break the mushrooms into smaller pieces or slice into ¼-inch-thick slices. Heat a large sauté pan over high heat. Add 1 tablespoon of the olive oil and 1 tablespoon of the butter to the pan. As soon as the butter melts, scatter one-third of the mushrooms in the bottom of the pan. Cook the mushrooms until caramelized on all sides, 3 to 4 minutes. Season the mushrooms with a generous pinch of salt and some pepper. Remove the mushrooms from the sauté pan and drain on paper towels. Repeat this process 2 more times with the olive oil, the butter, and the remaining mushrooms.

Place 1 tablespoon of the olive oil and 1 tablespoon of the butter in a medium (3-quart) saucepan over medium-high heat. When the butter has melted, add the walnuts, oregano, rosemary, and a generous pinch of salt. Cook for 1 to 2 minutes. Add the sautéed mushrooms to the pan. Add the wine and cook until the wine has evaporated completely, 3 to 5 minutes. Add all 4 cups of stock. Bring the mixture to a boil and decrease the heat to medium-low. Cook until the liquid is reduced and thickened, 15 to 20 minutes. Decrease the heat to very low and keep warm while cooking the venison.

Line a baking sheet with a rack. Heat a large cast-iron skillet or sauté pan over high heat. Add the remaining 2 tablespoons olive oil to the pan. Gently place the venison roast in the pan. Cook undisturbed for 2 to 3 minutes, until the roast is golden brown on the bottom and easily releases from the pan. Gently rotate the roast to sear another side. Repeat until the roast is evenly browned on all sides. Decrease the heat to low. Continue cooking the roast, occasionally rotating and turning the meat, until the internal temperature registers 115°F. Remove the meat from the hot pan and place on the prepared baking sheet. Let the roast rest at room temperature for 10 minutes.

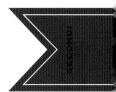

While the roast is resting, increase the heat under the mushroom mixture to medium-low. The mixture should be hot, but not simmering. Add the vinegar and the remaining 1 tablespoon butter to the mushroom mixture. Stir to combine. Taste and adjust the seasoning, if necessary.

Distribute the mushroom mixture among 4 warm serving plates or shallow bowls. Spoon any sauce in the pan over the mushrooms. Slice the venison into ¼-inch-thick slices. Distribute the slices on top of the mushrooms. Drizzle the meat with the high-quality extra-virgin olive oil. Serve with Maldon sea salt flakes on the side.

**NOTE:** "Denver" refers to the cut of the venison leg that is more tender than venison stew meat. If venison is unavailable, this dish can be made with beef tenderloin.

*Chapter 5*

# CONTORNI

*Contorni*—side dishes—is a category that appears on all of our restaurants' menus. I feel strongly that vegetables should be highlighted in every Italian meal—not to mention that they are one of my favorite things to cook.

When cooking vegetables, I have a couple of rules that I like to follow. First, it is important not to cook too many vegetables all at once. Vegetables have a high water content and tend to steam if they are crowded together in the pan. By cooking the vegetables in smaller batches, it is easier to achieve the caramelization that makes them sweet and delicious. Second, when in doubt, a little lemon juice can make all the difference. As when you're making a salad, cooked vegetables need to be dressed with the right amount of seasoning and acidity.

Although all of the *contorni* at our restaurants are served hot, I sometimes think that the flavors are even more pronounced when the dishes are served at room temperature. Feel free to make any of these dishes ahead of time and then let them rest on the table until you're ready to dig in.

*—Gabriel Thompson*

CONTORNI

# CANDIED PARSNIPS
# WITH HAZELNUTS

Parsnips are significantly sweeter than carrots. Thinly sliced and caramelized with a touch of honey, they are impossible to resist—in fact, once you start eating them, it is hard to stop.

*Pair with*
ROASTED
DUCK

## SERVES 4

3 tablespoons unsalted butter

4½ tablespoons extra-virgin olive oil

1 pound parsnips, peeled and sliced diagonally ⅛ inch thick (about 4½ cups)

Kosher salt

6 tablespoons roughly chopped blanched hazelnuts (or roughly chopped raw almonds)

4½ teaspoons honey

Line a baking sheet with paper towels. Place 1 tablespoon of the butter and 1½ tablespoons of the olive oil in a large sauté pan over high heat. When hot, add one-third (1½ cups) of the parsnips to the pan. Season the parsnips with a large pinch of salt. Toss together and sauté for 2 minutes. Add 2 tablespoons of the hazelnuts and 1½ teaspoons of the honey. Cook for 2 minutes more, stirring occasionally. When the parsnips are lightly golden brown, transfer the contents of the pan to the prepared baking sheet. Repeat this process 2 more times with the remaining ingredients. Taste and adjust the seasonings as needed.

Transfer the parsnips to a serving platter and serve immediately. Or place the baking sheet in a warm oven (200°F) until ready to serve.

# GRILLED SUMMER BEANS WITH ROASTED CHILIES

Ideally, these beans should be cooked on a grill—they're spectacular that way. But if you don't have one, you can cook the beans under a broiler instead. A grill pan or cast-iron skillet works well, too; just make sure the pan is crazy hot and you cook the beans in batches so that they char evenly.

*Pair with*
ROASTED
PORK LOIN

## SERVES 4 TO 6

4 red jalapeño chilies

½ cup plus
   1 tablespoon extra-
   virgin olive oil

½ teaspoon kosher
   salt, plus more
   for seasoning

2 tablespoons
   minced shallots

1 tablespoon freshly
   grated lemon zest

3 tablespoons
   freshly squeezed
   lemon juice

2 pounds green and/
   or yellow wax beans

Place the oven rack in the top position and preheat the oven to 350°F. Cut the jalapeños in half lengthwise and remove the stems and seeds. Place them, cut side down, on a baking sheet. Drizzle with the 1 tablespoon olive oil and season with salt. Roast in the oven until very tender and slightly blistered, 30 to 40 minutes.

Finely mince the roasted chilies and place in a small bowl. Add the shallots, lemon zest, lemon juice, the ½ teaspoon salt, and the ¼ cup of the olive oil. Stir and set aside. The roasted chili dressing can be made several hours in advance; cover and keep refrigerated until ready to use.

Bring a large pot of water to a boil. Season the water generously with salt (fresh beans need a lot of salt to make sure that they are properly seasoned); taste the water to make sure it is salty, like the sea. Cook the beans until tender (without a crunch), 5 to 7 minutes. Remove the beans from the water with a slotted spoon and place on a baking sheet or plate. Let the beans sit at room temperature until cool, or place in the refrigerator to speed up the cooling process. They can even rest in the refrigerator until you're ready to grill.

Preheat the grill to high heat. In a large bowl, toss the beans with the remaining ¼ cup olive oil and season with salt. When the grill is hot, spread the beans out onto the grill. Cook until the beans are charred and blistered on all sides, 5 to 7 minutes, depending on the heat of the grill.

Place the grilled beans in a large serving bowl. Add the roasted chili dressing and toss to combine. Taste and add more salt if necessary. Serve warm or at room temperature.

CONTORNI

# DELICATA SQUASH WITH SAGE

Originally, we served this with the chicken *al Diavolo* (see page 117) at dell'anima; the delicate sweetness of the squash works well next to the smoked paprika in the chicken. But this would also be the perfect side dish for Thanksgiving dinner—throw out the recipe for candied yams and serve this instead. Delicata squash is only in season in the fall (see Note), so I look forward to adding this dish to our menus every year.

*Pair with*
TURKEY OR
CHICKEN AL
DIAVOLO

## SERVES 4

2 delicata squash (about 1½ pounds, total)

4 teaspoons unsalted butter

2 tablespoons extra-virgin olive oil

½ teaspoon kosher salt

Freshly cracked black pepper

2 teaspoons honey or maple syrup

2 tablespoons torn fresh sage leaves

Preheat the oven to 350°F. Use a chef's knife to cut off and discard both ends of the squash. Cut the squash in half lengthwise. Use a spoon to scoop out and discard the seeds and pulp. Slice each squash half into ⅓- to ½-inch-thick half-moons.

Place 2 teaspoons of the butter and 1 tablespoon of the olive oil in a medium or large sauté pan over high heat. As soon as the butter has melted, add half of the squash. Season with ¼ teaspoon of the salt and several turns of black pepper. Drizzle with 1 teaspoon of the honey and sprinkle with 1 tablespoon of the sage leaves. Toss all of the ingredients together.

Using tongs or a spatula, distribute the squash pieces evenly so that 1 side of each half-moon is lying flat in the pan. Cook undisturbed until the bottom side of the squash is golden brown, about 3 minutes. Gently turn the squash pieces over; cook the other side until golden brown, about 2 minutes more. Transfer the squash pieces to a baking sheet. Return the pan to the heat and repeat this process with the remaining ingredients.

Distribute the squash evenly on the baking sheet. Place in the oven and roast until the squash is fork-tender, about 10 minutes. Taste and adjust the seasoning, if necessary.

**NOTE:** If delicata squash is not available, you can use sweet potatoes (leave the skins on; they keep the potatoes intact as they cook) or acorn, sweet dumpling, or butternut squash. One of the great things about delicata squash is that the skin is edible. The same is true for acorn and sweet dumpling squash. However, be sure to remove the inedible skin of butternut squash.

# ROASTED PEPPERS WITH ALMONDS AND PARMESAN

A few years ago, I visited Sycamore Farms at the Union Square Greenmarket and was blown away by their selection of bell peppers. I bought all of the peppers that were available. That night they appeared on L'Artusi's menu as a deconstructed romesco sauce: roasted peppers tossed in a crunchy almond pesto.

Pair with GRILLED STEAK, LAMB, OR SWORDFISH

**SERVES 6**

8 large red and yellow bell peppers, stems and seeds removed, sliced into ½-inch-wide strips

¼ cup plus 3 tablespoons extra-virgin olive oil

1 teaspoon kosher salt, plus more for seasoning

7 garlic cloves

2 tablespoons fresh oregano leaves

½ cup whole almonds

2 tablespoons freshly squeezed lemon juice

¼ cup freshly grated Parmesan cheese

Preheat the broiler to high. In a large bowl, toss the peppers with the ¼ cup olive oil and several pinches of salt. Spread the peppers out on a baking sheet. Broil, stirring occasionally, until slightly blackened on the edges, 15 to 20 minutes. Place the roasted peppers in a large bowl.

Meanwhile, place the garlic, oregano, almonds, and the 1 teaspoon salt in a mini food processor. Chop finely, occasionally scraping the sides of the container. The mixture will look like pesto without the oil.

Place the 3 tablespoons olive oil and the garlic-almond mixture in a large sauté pan over high heat. Cook, stirring constantly with a wooden spoon, until the garlic and almonds are slightly toasted and aromatic, about 3 minutes. The contents of the pan will have a tendency to stick to the bottom of the pan. Be sure to scrape the bottom of the pan with the wooden spoon so that the garlic does not burn. Once toasted, remove from the heat and add the almond mixture to the peppers.

Toss the peppers with the hot almond mixture, the lemon juice, and Parmesan. Taste and add more salt, if necessary. Serve hot or at room temperature.

# SUGAR SNAP PEAS WITH CHILIES AND MINT

Think of this as an Italian take on Chinese stir-fry. In fact, feel free to cook the entire recipe at once in a large wok, if you've got one. These peas take almost no time to cook, and their sweetness works beautifully against the hint of spiciness from the chili puree. Plus peas and mint are the perfect marriage.

*Pair with*
ARCTIC CHAR
OR SALMON

## SERVES 4

1 pound sugar snap peas

8 garlic cloves

2 tablespoons extra-virgin olive oil

Kosher salt

½ cup torn fresh mint leaves

2 tablespoons water

Freshly squeezed juice of 1 lemon

¼ to ½ teaspoon crushed Calabrian hot chili peppers

Remove and discard the stem end and string from each sugar snap pod. Slice the garlic cloves in half lengthwise and use a paring knife to gently remove the germ in the center of each half. Thinly slice the garlic lengthwise.

In a large sauté pan, heat 1 tablespoon of the olive oil over high heat. When the oil is hot, add half of the peas and season generously with salt. Toss the peas and spread them out to form a single layer in the pan. Cook undisturbed until the peas start to caramelize on the bottom, 1 to 2 minutes.

Add half of the garlic and toss to combine; then add half of the mint and toss to combine. Add 1 tablespoon of the water. Cook briefly until the water evaporates, about 1 minute. Transfer the contents of the pan to a bowl and set the bowl aside.

Return the pan to the stove and repeat this process with the remaining 1 tablespoon olive oil, the remaining peas, garlic, and mint, and the remaining 1 tablespoon water; but instead of transferring the cooked peas to the bowl, take the sauté pan off the heat and add the peas in the bowl to the sauté pan. Add the lemon juice and ¼ teaspoon of the crushed chili peppers; toss. Taste and add more salt and/or crushed chili peppers, if desired. Serve immediately.

CONTORNI

# SUMMER CORNTORNI

This started out as an inside joke—morphing the word *contorni* into corn*torni*. It's actually an Italian take on the classic Mexican corn dish *elote*, in which corn on the cob is slathered with mayonnaise, *queso fresco*, dried chilies, and lime. With a few liberal substitutions and by adding Parmesan, I figured it would pass as semi-Italian. Whether or not it is authentic, it is unbelievably delicious.

*Pair with*
ROASTED
WHITE FISH OR
BARBECUED
OR FRIED
CHICKEN

## SERVES 4

4 ears of fresh corn

2 scallions

2 tablespoons extra-virgin olive oil

1 tablespoon thinly sliced lemon zest

½ teaspoon plus 1 pinch of kosher salt, plus more as needed

¼ cup torn fresh basil leaves

2 tablespoons Greek yogurt

2 tablespoons freshly grated Parmesan cheese

½ teaspoon piment d'Espellete (see Note), plus more as needed

1 teaspoon freshly squeezed lemon juice

Remove the husks and silk from the corn. Using a chef's knife, slice the corn kernels off each cob and place in a bowl. Working over the bowl, scrape the cob with the back of the chef's knife to capture the juice and pulp.

Slice off and discard the ends and tough outer layers of the scallions. Cut the scallions in half where the white part meets the green part. Slice the white halves of the scallions in half lengthwise, then thinly slice each half crosswise into half-moons. Set aside. Thinly slice the green halves of the scallions diagonally. Set aside separately from the white parts of the scallions.

In a large sauté pan, combine the olive oil, the white parts of the scallions, the lemon zest, and the 1 pinch of salt. Place over high heat. Cook, stirring frequently, for 1 to 2 minutes. Add the sliced green scallions and sauté for 1 to 2 minutes. Add the corn kernels with juice and pulp. Season with the ½ teaspoon salt; toss and cook for 2 to 3 minutes more.

Remove the pan from the heat and add the basil, yogurt, Parmesan, *piment d'Espellete*, and lemon juice. Stir and taste, adjusting the seasoning as needed. Serve immediately.

**NOTE:** I was first introduced to *piment d'Espellete* while working at Le Bernardin. I fell in love with the spice: It is a pulverized dried pepper from the Basque region in France and Spain and has a slightly sweet flavor with a hint of spiciness. It is best served uncooked or used as a finishing pepper for dishes. Look for it at specialty spice stores or online. If it's unavailable, add a pinch of red chili flakes while sautéing the scallions.

CONTORNI

# BRUSSELS SPROUTS WITH PECORINO, LEMON, AND CRACKED PEPPER

With thinly sliced Brussels sprouts sautéed quickly and tossed in a lemony pepper dressing, this dish is similar to a warm slaw. Add an extra few turns of cracked black pepper—the spiciness works well next to the sprouts and the salty pecorino. If there are leftovers, incorporate them into a roasted pork or bacon sandwich.

*Pair with*
ROASTED CHICKEN

**SERVES 4 TO 6**

1 pound Brussels sprouts

4½ tablespoons extra-virgin olive oil

2 shallots, thinly sliced

Kosher salt

Freshly cracked black pepper

1½ tablespoons freshly squeezed lemon juice

3 tablespoons freshly grated Pecorino Romano cheese

Trim and discard the ends and tough outer leaves of the Brussels sprouts. Cut the sprouts in half lengthwise, then thinly slice lengthwise into a chiffonade.

Heat 1½ tablespoons of the olive oil in a large sauté pan over high heat. Add one-third of the shallots and a generous pinch of salt. Sauté for 1 to 2 minutes, until the shallots are slightly soft. Add one-third of the Brussels sprouts, another generous pinch of salt, and several turns of black pepper. Sauté, stirring and tossing frequently, for 2 to 3 minutes. The Brussels sprouts will turn bright green and will be slightly wilted, while retaining a bit of crunch.

Remove the Brussels sprouts from the pan and set aside in a large bowl. Repeat this process 2 more times with the remaining 3 tablespoons olive oil and the remaining shallots and sprouts.

Add the lemon juice and grated Pecorino Romano to the warm Brussels sprouts mixture. Toss to combine. Taste and adjust the seasoning, if necessary. This can be served warm or at room temperature.

# ROASTED CAULIFLOWER WITH CURRANTS, CAPERS, AND PINE NUTS

When roasting vegetables, I sometimes place the baking sheet in the oven during the preheating process. Once the oven and tray are very hot, I will then add the vegetables. I like to refer to this as a "sheet-pan roast." Not only do the vegetables cook more quickly, but they also take on a beautiful golden color. If you forget this step (as I sometimes do), no need to worry. The cauliflower may just take a few more minutes in the oven.

*Pair with*
ROASTED PORK, CHICKEN, OR DUCK

## SERVES 4

1 large head cauliflower (about 2½ pounds), leaves and stems removed, separated into 1-inch florets

5 tablespoons extra-virgin olive oil

2 teaspoons plus ½ teaspoon kosher salt, plus more for seasoning

¼ teaspoon red chili flakes plus more for seasoning

1 cup small dice red onion

3 tablespoons dried currants (or ¼ cup dark raisins)

1 tablespoon capers, rinsed and finely chopped

¼ cup dry white wine, such as Pinot Grigio

¼ cup red wine vinegar

½ cup roughly chopped Italian flat-leaf parsley

¼ cup toasted pine nuts

Preheat the oven to 400°F. Place a baking sheet in the oven to get it hot.

In a large bowl, toss together the cauliflower florets with 4 tablespoons of the olive oil, the 2 teaspoons kosher salt, and the ¼ teaspoon red chili flakes. Remove the hot baking sheet from the oven. Scatter the cauliflower on the baking sheet and return the baking sheet to the oven. Roast the cauliflower until it is golden in color and tender, about 40 minutes.

Meanwhile, heat the remaining 1 tablespoon olive oil in a large sauté pan over medium-high heat. Add the onion, currants, capers, the ½ teaspoon of kosher salt, and a pinch of red chili flakes. Sauté the onion mixture until the onions are soft and they start to take on a slight golden color, 6 to 8 minutes. Add the wine and cook until the liquid has evaporated completely, about 2 minutes. Then add the vinegar and reduce slightly, 1 to 2 minutes. Turn off the heat.

In the sauté pan or in a large bowl, toss together the onion-currant mixture, the roasted cauliflower, parsley, and pine nuts. Taste and adjust the seasoning. Serve warm or at room temperature.

CONTORNI

*Chapter 6*

# DOLCI

To me, the last course of a meal should be the most memorable course. And ever since I was in high school—when I declared in my senior yearbook that I was going to be a pastry chef—there's been nothing I've wanted more than to create those memories.

In 2007, after working in the restaurant business in various capacities for five years, I finally got my chance with the opening of dell'anima. For the first time, I had complete creative freedom to mess around with all kinds of different dessert ideas—and to receive immediate feedback from the guests.

I also won the lottery by having Gabe and Joe by my side. Gabe pushed me to take advantage of seasonal ingredients and taught me not to shy away from acidity and salt. Joe introduced me to Italian traditions in food and beverages that I had never heard of. Without Joe, I never would have discovered that *affogato* (vanilla gelato "drowned" in espresso) is spectacularly more delicious with a shot of amaro poured on top.

As a pastry chef, I try to create dishes that have a playful balance between temperatures (hot and cold), textures (soft and crunchy), and taste (sweet and salty). In a world of foams and powders, I want my desserts to taste like something my mom would make—approachable, familiar, and absolutely delicious. I also like to reinterpret traditional Italian desserts or take a traditional American dessert and give it an Italian twist. But my number-one goal is to see our guests light up with happiness over the last course. In fact, when Gabe can't stop eating one of my desserts, I know that I've succeeded!

Here are a few key points to keep in mind when making these desserts:

**FIRST READ THE RECIPE ALL THE WAY THROUGH.** You want to make sure you have all the ingredients on hand; plus, recipes may require chilling times, or components may need to be prepared in advance.

**INVEST IN A KITCHEN SCALE.** Weighing ingredients is much more accurate than using volume measurements. And if you are going to increase a recipe, it is best to increase the amounts by weight instead of volume. At the restaurants, we use an Escali Primo scale (available at Bed Bath & Beyond, Amazon, and many other retailers).

DOLCI

**BUY A GOOD ICE CREAM MAKER.** A cheap model is likely to burn out quickly, so if you're going to make a lot of gelato, I recommend going with a higher-end model.

**TAKE ADVANTAGE OF YOUR MICROWAVE.** It makes it so easy to soften butter, melt chocolate, and warm up sauces; and dishes that retain moisture are perfect reheated in the microwave, such as a slice of Blueberry-Polenta Upside-Down Cake (page 194). Just be sure to adjust the setting to 50% power and check frequently.

**TASTE AS YOU GO.** I always taste batter and raw ingredients before cooking them (if I'm working with eggs, I use the freshest ones possible—and I take the risk). If it does not taste good in its raw state, then it will not taste good in the end. And you never know when you might forget an ingredient or accidentally mis-measure. It is better to catch mistakes sooner rather than later.

**USE THE RIGHT INGREDIENTS.** I use **large eggs,** and the recipes are developed with that in mind. Always use **unsalted butter,** which allows you to control the amount of salt in a dish. I prefer **organic cream and milk,** ideally from a local farm. For **chocolate and cocoa powder,** I prefer Valrhona. It is very consistent and not too sweet. Be sure to store it in a cool, dark, dry place. Chocolate can spoil quickly if not stored properly; it will lose its oily sheen, and the texture will be grainy and unappealing.

*—Katherine Thompson*

**On dessert wine pairings:** Other than biscotti dipped into nutty Vin Santo wine, it is rare in Italy to have a dessert wine with dessert. After-dinner sweets or fruit are eaten with espresso (Italians never have milk in their coffee after dinner) and sometimes a little *digestivo* after that (see page 215). However, Italy makes some truly amazing sweet wines, referred to as *vini da meditazione,* or "wines to think about." In this case the wines themselves become the main attraction and are served with a very simple dry crumbly cookie or cake or often nothing at all. Italian sweet wines range from the lightly sweet and frothy Moscato d'Asti and Brachetto d'Acqui to the rich, dense, powerful Recioto della Valpolicella, which is dark red, chocolaty, and delicious.

When pairing a wine with dessert, the traditional thinking is that you need the wine to be at least as sweet as the dessert; otherwise the dessert will overpower it. I reject that—you just end up with a mouth full of sugar. If you really want sweet wine with your dessert, I'd stick with the sparkling wines mentioned above. If it's a dessert that has chocolate or berries, try Brachetto d'Acqui. If it has stone fruit or none at all, then Moscato is the way to go. And if you have a good bottle of Vin Santo in the house, put the cookies on the side and sip the wine by itself.

*—Joe Campanale*

# FRUTTA AL FORNO

This recipe features baked peaches with a pecan crisp topping, but feel free to get creative with the ingredients depending on the season: strawberry and rhubarb, apple and cranberry, blueberries, plums. If the fruit is especially tart, you may want to add more sugar. Use whatever nuts you have on hand; or if you have a nut allergy, add extra oats in place of the nuts. Just be sure to eat this warm with a little vanilla gelato or—as my mom would suggest—drizzled with a tablespoon of very cold organic heavy cream.

**SERVES 6**

6 cups peeled and diced peaches

½ cup sugar

1½ tablespoons instant tapioca pudding (see Note)

Freshly squeezed juice of 1 lemon

1½ teaspoons vanilla extract

1 teaspoon kosher salt

¼ cup unbleached all-purpose flour

¼ cup pecan pieces (or walnuts, almonds, or hazelnuts)

2 tablespoons rolled oats

2 tablespoons light or dark brown sugar

1 ounce (2 tablespoons) cold unsalted butter, diced

⅛ teaspoon ground cinnamon

⅛ teaspoon ground nutmeg (optional)

Preheat the oven to 350°F. In a medium bowl, toss the peaches with the sugar, tapioca pudding, lemon juice, vanilla, and ¾ teaspoon of the salt. Pour into a 9½-inch pie plate or a shallow baking container that holds 2 quarts.

Place the flour, pecans, oats, brown sugar, butter, cinnamon, nutmeg, if using, and the remaining ¼ teaspoon salt in a food processor. Pulse until the mixture is crumbly. Scatter the nut topping all over the fruit mixture.

Bake until the mixture is bubbly, 50 minutes to 1 hour. Let cool for 1 hour before serving. The crisp can be made ahead of time and rewarmed in a 300°F oven for 5 to 10 minutes before serving, but it is best served the day that it is baked.

**NOTE:** Tapioca thickens fruit beautifully without the cloying quality that results from flour and other thickeners. If it's unavailable, you can substitute cornstarch. Or leave it out completely and enjoy the fruit crisp in bowls with a looser texture.

# BITTERSWEET CHOCOLATE BUDINO

Joe's mom, Karen Campanale (aka dell'animom), is a true chocolate lover; whenever she goes out to eat, Karen insists on ordering the chocolate dessert. Coming up with a dessert that satisfies a true chocolate lover is no small task. I knew I had succeeded with this *budino* (pudding)—a rich, creamy version of the classic *pot de crème*—when Karen came to L'Artusi's opening. She ordered the bittersweet chocolate *budino*, ate the entire dessert, then ordered another one and ate that, too.

**SERVES 6**

5½ ounces bittersweet chocolate (70% cacao), finely chopped

1 cup heavy cream

⅔ cup whole milk

⅓ cup sugar

¼ teaspoon kosher salt

4 large egg yolks

¾ teaspoon vanilla extract

Lightly sweetened whipped cream, for serving

Grated bittersweet chocolate, for garnish

**SPECIAL EQUIPMENT**

- 6 (3- TO 4-OUNCE) RAMEKINS

- ROASTING PAN

Preheat the oven to 275°F. Place the chocolate in a large bowl. Combine the cream, milk, sugar, and salt in a small (1-quart) saucepan and bring to a boil over medium heat. Immediately pour the hot cream mixture over the chocolate. Whisk to combine and then whisk some more. Walk away for 5 minutes. Whisk again. It is very important that the chocolate is thoroughly melted in the cream mixture.

Place the yolks in a medium bowl and whisk them lightly. Slowly pour the chocolate mixture into the egg yolks, whisking constantly. Add the vanilla and whisk to combine. Using a fine-mesh strainer, strain the chocolate mixture into another medium bowl. This will remove any bits of egg that have cooked too much.

Divide the chocolate custard among six 3- to 4-ounce ramekins. Place the ramekins in a roasting pan and fill the pan with enough water to come halfway up the sides of the ramekins. Cover the pan with foil. Bake in the water bath until the custard has just set, but still has a slight jiggle in the center, 40 to 50 minutes; check frequently toward the end of the cooking time, as the custards can transition quickly from underbaked to overbaked (with no jiggle).

Remove the ramekins from the water bath. Let the custards cool, then cover them individually with plastic wrap and refrigerate until chilled, several hours or overnight. Serve with whipped cream and garnish with grated chocolate.

# BUDINO DI RISO WITH CARAMELIZED BANANAS, BANANA-LIME SORBET, AND SESAME BRITTLE

There isn't a culture in the world that doesn't have its own version of rice pudding—and I'm thankful for that. I am infatuated with the chewiness of rice combined with the creaminess of a sweet sauce. This version is a little unusual, but I like to break the rules. Cardamom is not typically found in Italian cuisine, but the spice is undeniably good with bananas. And instead of a dry, sesame Italian cookie, I opted for a sweeter, crunchy sesame-brittle topping that's a great foil next to the creamy pudding. All of the components are great in one bite, but do not hesitate to eat the pudding on its own.

**SERVES 6**

½ cup arborio rice

2 cups whole milk

1 cup heavy cream

¼ cup plus
8 teaspoons sugar

¼ teaspoon kosher salt

2 cardamom pods

1 strip of lemon
peel (½ inch by
1½ inches)

½ vanilla bean, split
lengthwise

1 small bay leaf

2 bananas

Banana-Lime Sorbet
(page 207)

Sesame Brittle
(recipe follows)

Preheat the oven to 325°F. Bring a medium pot of water to a boil. Add the rice to the boiling water. Boil the rice for 2 minutes, then drain.

Place the rice in a small (2-quart) ovenproof saucepan. Add 1¾ cups of the milk, ¾ cup of the cream, the ¼ cup sugar, the salt, cardamom, lemon peel, vanilla bean, and bay leaf. Stirring occasionally, bring this mixture to a simmer. Cover the saucepan and place in the oven. Bake for 40 minutes.

Remove the cardamom pods, lemon peel, vanilla bean, and bay leaf. Pour the rice pudding into a shallow container, such as a pie plate, to cool. Stir occasionally to cool the pudding faster. When it reaches room temperature, add the remaining ¼ cup milk and the remaining ¼ cup heavy cream. Stir to combine. Store the pudding, covered, in the refrigerator for 1 to 2 days, until ready to serve.

To caramelize the bananas, preheat the broiler to high. Slice each banana in half crosswise, then in half again lengthwise; place the 8 pieces on a baking sheet. Sprinkle 1 teaspoon of the remaining sugar over each banana slice. Place under the broiler and cook until the sugar caramelizes and the bananas have dark roasted edges, 3 to 4 minutes. Be sure to rotate the pan to make sure that the bananas cook evenly. Alternatively, use a kitchen torch to caramelize the sugar on the banana slices.

To serve, place a ¼-cup to ⅓-cup scoop of rice pudding in each serving bowl. Distribute the warm, caramelized banana slices over the pudding (giving 2 servings an extra piece of banana, or slicing the extra pieces and distributing among the servings). Top each serving with a small scoop of banana-lime sorbet. Sprinkle with the sesame brittle and serve immediately.

## SESAME BRITTLE

In this preparation, sesame seeds are soaked in simple syrup. The simple syrup is drained off and the seeds are toasted in the oven with a sprinkle of salt. The seeds absorb just enough of the syrup to give them a hint of sweetness and a crunchy, brittle-like exterior. Since sesame seeds taste a lot like peanuts, this recipe is a slight twist on peanut brittle— and a lot easier to execute.

**MAKES ¼ TO ⅓ CUP**

| | | |
|---|---|---|
| ½ cup water | ¼ cup sesame seeds (white and black) | Pinch of kosher salt |
| ½ cup sugar | | |

Preheat the oven to 325°F. Line a baking sheet with parchment paper. Bring the water and sugar to a simmer in a small saucepan. Turn off the heat. Add the sesame seeds. Let the seeds sit in the simple syrup for 10 minutes. Drain the sesame seeds and distribute onto the prepared baking sheet. Sprinkle the seeds with a pinch of salt. Bake until the sesame seeds are toasted, 15 to 17 minutes. Remove from the oven and let cool to room temperature. Break up the sesame brittle by hand into small, crumbly pieces. The sesame brittle can be stored in an airtight container at room temperature for up to 1 week.

# IMPROMPTU TIRAMISU

Traditional tiramisu recipes require several steps: Usually there is an egg custard involved, and some even require making your own ladyfingers. The truth is, you can achieve the same flavors and texture with purchased ladyfingers (the texture and flavor of Savoiardi cookies are perfect) soaked in an espresso-rum mixture and layered with a simple mascarpone mousse. Chocolate wafers add a little more texture and give the recipe an icebox cake twist. Note that this tiramisu has a definite boozy kick!

**SERVES 4 TO 6**

1¼ cups heavy cream

½ cup fresh espresso or dark coffee

¼ cup plus 2 tablespoons dark rum

1 (1-pound) container of mascarpone

¼ cup coffee liqueur

¼ cup sugar

12 ladyfingers, roughly broken up into 1-inch pieces

12 chocolate wafers, chopped into coarse crumbs

Whip the cream until it holds soft peaks. Set aside in the refrigerator. In a small bowl, combine the espresso with the ¼ cup rum. Set aside.

In a large bowl, whisk the 2 tablespoons rum, the mascarpone, coffee liqueur, and sugar until smooth. Gradually fold in the whipped cream. Whisk slightly to remove any lumps. Do not overmix, or the mixture will turn to butter.

Place a single layer of ladyfingers on the bottom of a shallow medium (1½- to 2-quart) bowl or casserole dish. Drizzle the ladyfingers with half of the coffee-rum mixture. Spread half of the mascarpone cream on top of the ladyfingers. Sprinkle half of the chocolate wafer crumbs over the cream.

Layer the ladyfingers, coffee-rum mixture, and mascarpone cream 1 more time, reserving the remaining chocolate wafers. Freeze for 1 to 2 hours before serving. (The tiramisu can also be frozen in an airtight container for up to 2 weeks. Place in the refrigerator for 1 to 2 hours before serving.) Just before serving, sprinkle the tiramisu with the remaining chocolate wafers.

**NOTE:** I absolutely love Nabisco chocolate wafers. They are rich and chocolaty without being too sweet. If Nabisco chocolate wafers are hard to find, feel free to substitute another purchased chocolate wafer, such as cocoa tea biscuits.

# CHOCOLATE HAZELNUT TORTE

The combination of chocolate and hazelnuts is very popular in Italy (think of Baci candies and Nutella). Here is a gluten-free chocolate hazelnut cake that tastes like a rich, decadent brownie. Be sure to slightly underbake the cake; it will stay moist longer and will be easier to slice. Also, I recommend baking the cake a day ahead and chilling it thoroughly—a room-temperature cake can fall apart when you remove it from the cake pan, and the ganache will pour more easily over the chilled cake. Let the glazed cake sit at room temperature for 1 to 2 hours before serving. Because the cake is on the sweeter side, it's excellent garnished with unsweetened whipped cream.

**SERVES 8**

## TORTE

Nonstick vegetable oil spray

5 ounces (10 tablespoons) unsalted butter, softened

¾ cup sugar

4 large eggs

1 tablespoon plus 2 teaspoons dark or light rum

¾ teaspoon kosher salt

5 ounces bittersweet chocolate (70% cacao), melted

5 ounces (1¼ cups) finely ground toasted hazelnuts

## GLAZE

5 ounces bittersweet chocolate (70% cacao), coarsely chopped

2½ teaspoons honey

2½ ounces (5 tablespoons) unsalted butter, softened

Pinch of kosher salt

¼ cup roughly chopped or halved toasted hazelnuts, for garnish

For the torte, preheat the oven to 325°F. Spray an 8-inch cake pan with nonstick spray; line with parchment paper and spray again with nonstick spray.

In a stand mixer fitted with the paddle attachment, cream the butter and sugar on medium speed until well combined, about 2 minutes. Add the eggs, one at a time, scraping the sides of the bowl after each addition. Add the rum and salt, and mix to combine. Add the chocolate and hazelnuts. Mix until the batter looks homogeneous.

Pour the batter into the prepared pan and bake until a wooden skewer inserted into the center of the cake comes out with moist crumbs attached, 40 to 45 minutes.

Let the cake cool, then place in the refrigerator for a few hours or, preferably, overnight before unmolding.

For the glaze, melt the chocolate in a double boiler or in the microwave on medium power. When the chocolate is melted and hot to the touch, stir in the honey, butter, and salt. Reheat the mixture for a few seconds and make sure the butter is fully incorporated into the chocolate.

With a serrated paring knife, cut any crusty pieces off the top of the cake. Invert the cake onto an 8-inch round piece of cardboard (the flat bottom of the cake should now be on top). Place the cake on a rack on a baking sheet or sheet of parchment paper. Gently pour the warm chocolate glaze all over the torte. Use an offset spatula to spread the glaze evenly over the top and sides of the cake. Lightly tap the rack to remove any bubbles and to smooth out the glaze. Let the cake sit for 15 to 30 minutes at room temperature, until the glaze just begins to set. The torte can be glazed and kept covered in the refrigerator for 1 day before serving.

On the day that the cake will be served, garnish the cake decoratively with the toasted hazelnuts. Let the cake sit at room temperature for several hours before serving.

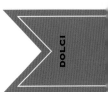

# CRÈME FRAÎCHE PANNA COTTA WITH SEMOLINA SHORTBREAD, VANILLA-MACERATED STRAWBERRIES, AND SABA

Panna cotta, or "cooked cream," is a classic Italian dessert consisting of sweetened milk "cooked" with gelatin. I am panna cotta's harshest critic. Usually the dessert is made with too much gelatin and the milk has a watery texture. To me, that is a waste of calories. I prefer panna cotta made with the least amount of gelatin possible—each bite should be silky smooth. Be sure to plan in advance: Gelatin requires several hours to solidify. Either make the panna cotta in the morning or the day before you plan to serve it.

## SERVES 6

### PANNA COTTA

1½ cups heavy cream

1 teaspoon powdered gelatin

6 tablespoons sugar

1¼ cups crème fraîche or sour cream

½ teaspoon vanilla extract

½ teaspoon kosher salt

### STRAWBERRIES

1 quart strawberries, stems removed, thinly sliced

1 vanilla bean, split in half lengthwise, seeds scraped out

Freshly squeezed juice of 1 lemon

2 tablespoons sugar

Pinch of kosher salt

### ASSEMBLY

6 semolina shortbread cookies (recipe follows)

2 tablespoons Saba (see Note)

## SPECIAL EQUIPMENT

• 6 (4-OUNCE) PANNA COTTA MOLDS

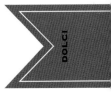

For the panna cotta, place ¼ cup of the cream in a small bowl. Sprinkle with the powdered gelatin. Let sit for 5 to 10 minutes to soften, then stir with a fork to break up any clumps.

In a small (2-quart) saucepan, heat the remaining 1¼ cups cream and the sugar over low heat. Add the gelatin mixture to the hot cream mixture. Stir to combine and to melt the gelatin; do not boil.

# CRÈME FRAÎCHE PANNA COTTA
**CONTINUED**

Place the crème fraîche, vanilla, and salt in a large bowl. Pour the hot cream mixture over the crème fraîche mixture. Whisk together until smooth. Pour the mixture into 6 individual 4-ounce panna cotta molds or ramekins. Let cool; cover with plastic wrap and refrigerate overnight.

For the strawberries, combine the strawberries, vanilla bean pod and seeds, lemon juice, sugar, and salt in a medium bowl. Let sit at room temperature for 30 minutes. Refrigerate until ready to serve; the strawberries are best served the same day. Remove vanilla bean pod before serving.

To assemble, just before serving, gently warm the outsides of the panna cotta molds under warm water to loosen.

Place 1 semolina shortbread cookie on each serving plate. Unmold 1 panna cotta on top of each cookie. The cookie will act like a crust for the dessert. Distribute some strawberries and their juices next to each panna cotta. Drizzle a scant teaspoon of Saba next to the strawberries. Serve immediately.

**NOTE:** Saba is an Italian condiment made from the grape must of Lambrusco and Trebbiano grapes. It is similar to balsamic vinegar, but thicker, sweeter, and with a more caramelized flavor. Saba is available at Italian specialty stores and can be purchased over the Internet. If it's unavailable, balsamic vinegar reduced by half can be substituted. When using Saba, be aware that it has an intense flavor; a little bit goes a long way. Saba is also a great condiment for funky cheeses and roast duck or pork.

# SEMOLINA SHORTBREAD

These thin, buttery cookies act as a crust under the panna cotta, similar to a cheesecake crust. This recipe makes plenty for other uses; they are delicious served with macerated citrus and sabayon, with sorbet—or all on their own. And the dough freezes beautifully, so you can have cookies any time you want.

**MAKES 3 DOZEN**

8 ounces (2 sticks) unsalted butter, softened

¾ cup sugar

¾ teaspoon kosher salt

Finely grated zest of ½ lemon

¼ teaspoon vanilla extract

1 large egg

2 cups plus 2 tablespoons unbleached all-purpose flour

¾ cup semolina flour (or substitute instant polenta)

**SPECIAL EQUIPMENT**

- 1 (3-INCH) ROUND COOKIE CUTTER

In a stand mixer fitted with the paddle attachment, cream the butter, sugar, salt, and lemon zest on medium speed for about 1 minute. Add the vanilla and egg. Cream until smooth, scraping down the sides of the bowl occasionally. Add the flour and semolina. Mix on low speed until just combined.

Divide the dough in half. Roll out 1 of the dough halves between 2 pieces of parchment paper until ⅛ to ¼ inch thick. Remove the top piece of parchment paper. Use a round 3-inch cookie cutter or a highball glass to cut cookies that will fit under the base of the panna cotta molds, but do not remove the dough rounds, or the excess dough, from the paper. Replace the top sheet of parchment paper and place the dough, between the pieces of parchment paper, in the freezer on a baking sheet. Repeat with the second half of the dough.

After 15 to 20 minutes, remove the trays from the freezer and remove the top layer of parchment paper. Preheat the oven to 350°F. With a small knife, remove the excess dough surrounding the circles. Space the cookies evenly on the baking sheets (still lined with parchment paper) and set aside for baking. Feel free to re-roll the excess dough and repeat the process to make more cookies while you bake the first batch.

Place one baking sheet on the middle rack and the other on the lower rack. Bake the cookie rounds, switching the baking sheets and rotating each 180 degrees halfway through the cooking time, until the edges are slightly golden and the centers are a pale yellow, 12 to 13 minutes. Gently transfer the cookies to a rack and let cool. Store in an airtight container until ready to serve.

# GOAT CHEESE MOUSSE WITH HONEY-ROASTED FIGS AND PINE NUT CRISPS

When fresh figs appear in the late summer or early fall, I am immediately reminded of Caravaggio's still life paintings featuring this beautiful, sensual fruit. You can taste the sweetness just by looking at them. To offset the sweetness of the figs, I like to serve them with a barely sweetened, tangy goat cheese mousse. The crispy pine nut cookie works well next to the softness of the mousse and fruit. Gabe likes to spread the mousse on the cookie and place the figs on top; feel free to attack the components however you like.

## SERVES 4 TO 6

4 ounces goat cheese

¼ cup plus 2 tablespoons simple syrup (see page 12)

¼ teaspoon kosher salt, plus more for sprinkling

½ cup heavy cream

½ teaspoon vanilla extract

5 to 7 fresh figs

1 tablespoon honey

Freshly squeezed juice of ½ lemon

4 to 6 Pine Nut Crisps (recipe follows)

Place the goat cheese, the ¼ cup simple syrup, and the salt in a small saucepan. Place over low heat and cook, stirring frequently, until the goat cheese melts and the mixture looks homogeneous, 2 to 4 minutes. Remove from the heat and place the melted goat cheese in a medium bowl. Set aside and let cool to room temperature, 10 to 15 minutes.

Whisk the cream and vanilla until medium peaks form. Gradually fold the whipped cream into the goat cheese. Place the goat cheese mousse in an airtight container and store refrigerated until ready to serve. The mousse can be made 2 to 3 hours ahead.

Preheat the oven to 350°F. Cut the stems off the figs. Slice each fig lengthwise into quarters. Place the fig quarters in a small, ovenproof saucepan, skin side down. Drizzle the figs with the 2 tablespoons simple syrup, the honey, and lemon juice. Sprinkle the figs with a pinch of salt. Roast the figs in the oven, uncovered, for 18 to 20 minutes.

To serve, place a dollop, or quenelle, of goat cheese mousse on each dessert plate or shallow bowl. Distribute the figs next to the mousse. Drizzle some of the liquid from the figs onto the plate. Garnish with a pine nut crisp.

# PINE NUT CRISPS

I'm a sucker for anything with layers of phyllo dough, such as baklava. This delicate dough is tender, flaky, and easy to use. Here it is layered with chopped pine nuts and sugar and baked long enough to caramelize the sugar to give the cookies a crisp texture. Feel free to substitute another nut instead of pine nuts, or leave the nuts out altogether.

## MAKES 16 COOKIES

5 (9- by 14-inch) sheets of phyllo dough

2 ounces (4 tablespoons) unsalted butter, melted

5 teaspoons sugar

¼ cup finely chopped pine nuts

Preheat the oven to 350°F. Place 1 sheet of phyllo dough on a piece of parchment paper or a Silpat liner. Brush the phyllo dough lightly with some of the melted butter. Sprinkle 1 teaspoon of sugar evenly over the dough. Sprinkle 1 tablespoon of pine nuts over the dough. Place another sheet of phyllo over the pine nuts. Repeat this layering process 4 more times (the last layer of dough will just have butter and sugar, no nuts).

To clean up the sides, cut and discard the very outer edges of the phyllo rectangle; be sure not to cut through the parchment paper or Silpat. Cut the dough in half lengthwise. Then cut the dough crosswise into 4 pieces (at this point, the dough will be divided into 8 rectangles). Cut each rectangle diagonally in half to create 16 triangular pieces. Slide the parchment paper or Silpat with the cookies onto a baking sheet.

Lay another piece of parchment paper or Silpat over the cookies and weigh it down with another baking sheet. Bake the cookies until they are golden brown, 15 to 18 minutes. Immediately remove the top baking sheet and top layer of parchment paper or Silpat. Transfer the cookies to a cooling rack. When cool, place in an airtight container with parchment paper between the cookie layers. The cookies will last 2 to 3 days in an airtight container.

# FRUTTI DI BOSCO SUNDAE

This is an Italian take on the classic English dessert Eton Mess: a mash-up of strawberries, whipped cream, and meringue—three of my favorite dessert components. Instead of limiting myself to strawberries, I like to add any sort of fruit or berry that I can get my hands on during the summer months. In the height of the season, the frutti di bosco (Italian for "fruits of the forest") can include blackberries, raspberries, cherries, red currants, and, of course, strawberries. Brachetto d'Acqui is the perfect match for these fruits. This slightly sweet, sparkling red wine from Piedmont complements the color of the berries and gives the fruit an aromatic, floral flavor. The sundae is delicious on its own or paired with the Anise Pizzelle Cookies (see page 203).

## SERVES 4 TO 6

3 cups mixed berries (raspberries, blackberries, strawberries, cherries, blueberries, currants)

⅓ cup Brachetto or Prosecco (or 2 tablespoons freshly squeezed lemon juice)

2 tablespoons granulated sugar

1 vanilla bean, split

Pinch of kosher salt

2 cups heavy cream

2 tablespoons confectioners' sugar

Raspberry Sorbet (page 209)

Meringue Kisses (recipe follows)

**SPECIAL EQUIPMENT**

• PASTRY BAG

• 4 TO 6 HIGHBALL OR SUNDAE GLASSES

Remove the stems and seeds from the fruit. Slice any large fruit into smaller pieces. Set aside 1 cup of the fresh fruit to use as a garnish.

Toss the remaining 2 cups fruit with the sparkling wine, sugar, vanilla bean, and salt. Let sit at room temperature for 15 to 30 minutes. You can store the macerated fruit in the refrigerator for up to 4 hours. Remove the vanilla bean before serving.

Whip the cream and confectioners' sugar to medium peaks. For ease, place the whipped cream in a pastry bag or plastic bag with 1 corner snipped off. Pipe small amounts of the whipped cream into individual chilled highball or sundae glasses.

Place a small scoop of raspberry sorbet on the whipped cream in each glass. Top with a generous amount of the macerated fruit and some of the liquid from the fruit. Place 3 or 4 meringue kisses on the fruit. If there is room in the glass, feel free to repeat this layering process.

Garnish the top of each sundae with additional whipped cream, some of the reserved fresh fruit, and a few more meringue kisses. Serve immediately.

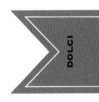

# FRUTTI DI BOSCO SUNDAE
**CONTINUED**

# MERINGUE KISSES

This recipe makes a large amount of meringue kisses—it is hard to scale down the recipe, because you need enough volume of egg whites in order for the whisk attachment to reach the egg whites! If desired, pipe the amount of kisses that you need for the recipe, then experiment with the rest of the meringue mixture. For example, pipe it into large disks to make pavlova. Or fold in chopped toasted nuts and/or chopped chocolate and mound into larger shapes to make a completely different cookie. Be sure to store the cooked meringues in an airtight container in a cool, dry place; they'll keep for 1 to 2 weeks. Humidity is the kiss of death for meringue.

**MAKES 12 DOZEN**

| | | |
|---|---|---|
| 3 large egg whites, at room temperature | ½ cup granulated sugar | ⅔ cup confectioners' sugar, sifted |

**SPECIAL EQUIPMENT**

- **PASTRY BAG WITH STAR TIP**

Preheat the oven to 225°F. Line 2 baking sheets with Silpat liners or parchment paper.

With a stand mixer fitted with the wire whisk attachment, whisk the egg whites on medium speed until frothy. Slowly add the granulated sugar, 1 tablespoon at a time. After all of the granulated sugar has been added, increase the speed to high and whip until the mixture forms stiff peaks. Do not overmix, or the meringue will appear dry.

Remove the bowl from the mixer. Fold in the confectioners' sugar. Spoon the egg white mixture into a pastry bag fitted with a star tip.

Pipe the meringue into ¾-inch kisses onto the prepared baking sheets, spacing the kisses 1½ to 2 inches apart. Bake the kisses for 35 to 40 minutes. Remove 1 kiss from the oven. Let cool for 2 to 3 minutes. Break the kiss in half. If it is dry all the way through, the kisses are done baking. If the kiss is moist in the center, let the kisses bake for 5 to 10 minutes more and test again. The kisses should be crunchy, dry, and white in color. Remove the kisses from the oven. As soon as they are cool (approximately 15 minutes), immediately transfer the kisses to an airtight container. Store in a dry place at room temperature. They can be made several days in advance.

# CARAMELIZED POACHED PEARS WITH CRESPELLE

I have Julia Child to thank for this dessert. When I was twelve, my grandmother helped me make Julia's classic French dessert, poached pears with puff pastry, pastry cream, and caramel sauce. We made everything from scratch (even the puff pastry) and to this day I remember it as one of the best desserts I've ever had. I wanted to put an Italian twist on it, while simplifying the process a little. The result was mascarpone-stuffed crepes with pears poached in Moscato d'Asti, a delicious dessert wine from Piedmont. If desired, garnish with a dollop of crème fraîche mousse (see page 191) and sprinkle with crushed amaretti cookies. Save the poaching liquid to make an incredible mocktail with sparkling water and a twist of lemon. Or booze it up with a little pear brandy.

## SERVES 6

1 bottle Moscato d'Asti

2 cups sugar

2 strips of lemon zest, peeled with a vegetable peeler (½ by 1½ inches)

1 bay leaf

1 vanilla bean, split lengthwise

3 Bosc or Anjou pears

¼ cup water

6 Crespelle (crepes; recipe follows)

6 tablespoons mascarpone or cream cheese, softened

1 ounce (2 tablespoons) unsalted butter, softened

Place the Moscato, 1½ cups of the sugar, the lemon zest, bay leaf, and vanilla bean in a medium (3-quart) saucepan.

Using a vegetable peeler, peel each pear from the stem to the bottom core. Using a paring knife, cut each stem in half (see Note), then use a chef's knife to cut each pear in half lengthwise. Use a melon baller or teaspoon measure to remove the center core and seeds in a circle. With a paring knife, cut out the bottom core and the top core, leaving the stem area intact. Place the pears in the Moscato liquid as they are being prepared.

Cover the pears with a round of parchment paper to keep the pears submerged in the liquid. Place the saucepan over medium heat. Do not cover the saucepan with a lid; you do not want the mixture to come to a boil. Bring to a simmer, then turn the heat down to low. Poach the pears for 30 to 45 minutes, keeping the poaching liquid just under a simmer the entire time, until the pears are easily pierced with a metal skewer and are translucent all the way through. (The cooking time will vary depending on the ripeness of the pears.)

# CARAMELIZED POACHED PEARS WITH CRESPELLE
**CONTINUED**

When the pears are ready, remove them with a slotted spoon and let cool in a bowl or on a plate. Set aside ½ cup plus 2 tablespoons of the poaching liquid to finish the pears. When the pears and the poaching liquid are cool, transfer the pears to an airtight container and pour the remainder of the poaching liquid over them. Store refrigerated in the airtight container. The poached pears can be made 3 to 4 days in advance.

To serve the pears, preheat the oven to 350°F. Place the ¼ cup water and the remaining ½ cup sugar in a small sauté pan over medium-low heat. Slowly cook the sugar-water mixture until the sugar turns a dark-amber caramel. Remove the pan from the heat and slowly add the reserved pear poaching liquid. Return the pan to low heat and use a heatproof spatula or a wooden spoon to stir the caramel and poaching liquid.

Meanwhile, drain the pears and use a paring knife to slice the pears ¼ inch thick on the diagonal lengthwise from the bottom nearly to the top, leaving the stem area intact; the pears will fan out at the bottom. Gently lay the pears in the hot caramel liquid. Place on low heat while preparing the *crespelle*.

Spread 1 tablespoon of the mascarpone on the bottom half of each crepe. Fold the top half of the crepe over the cheese mixture. Fold in half again to create a triangle. Place on a baking sheet. Once all of the crepes are arranged, spread 1 teaspoon of softened butter on each triangle. Place in the oven for 5 to 10 minutes, until the crepes are warm.

To serve, place each crepe on a small plate or in a shallow bowl. Gently place a pear half on each crepe. Spoon 1 to 2 tablespoons of the caramel poaching liquid over each pear. Serve immediately.

**NOTE:** I like to preserve the pear stems because it makes for an elegant presentation, but if the stems don't cooperate, you can also simply remove them.

# CRESPELLE

Although crepes are known as a French specialty, they are also served all over Italy, where they're called *crespelle*. This is Julia Child's crepe recipe—but with a bonus trick from my husband: browning the butter before adding it to the batter. This gives the *crespelle* a beautiful golden color and incorporates a nutty flavor into the batter. Do not get discouraged if the first crepe doesn't look perfect; just eat it as you practice with the rest of the batter. *Crespelle* can also be made in advance and stored in the refrigerator or freezer.

## MAKES 6 TO 7 (7-INCH) CREPES

1 large egg

1 large egg yolk

¼ cup water

¼ cup milk

½ cup unbleached
all-purpose flour

1 tablespoon sugar

¼ teaspoon kosher salt

1 tablespoon dark
or light rum

¾ ounce
(1½ tablespoons)
plus 2 tablespoons
unsalted butter

**SPECIAL EQUIPMENT**

• 1 (7-INCH)
SKILLET OR CREPE
PAN

In a medium bowl, whisk the egg, egg yolk, water, and milk. Add the flour, sugar, and salt. Whisk until smooth. Slowly whisk in the rum. Melt the ¾ ounce butter in a small saucepan over medium-low heat. Cook until the butter is brown and aromatic. Pour directly into the crepe batter and whisk to combine. Place the batter in an airtight container and store in the refrigerator for 30 minutes to 1 hour.

Heat a nonstick 7-inch skillet or crepe pan over medium heat. When the pan is hot, decrease the heat to low. Add 1 teaspoon of the remaining butter to the pan and use a paper towel to rub the butter all over the bottom of the pan. Add 2 tablespoons of batter to the pan and slowly turn the pan to distribute the batter evenly over the bottom. Cook over low heat for 1 to 2 minutes, until there is a hint of golden color on the bottom of the crepe. Use a spatula to loosen the edges. Then using your fingertips, pinch one side of the crepe and flip it over to the other side. Cook for another 30 seconds, until the bottom is set. Remove the crepe from the pan and set aside on a plate. Repeat with the rest of the batter, stacking the cooked crepes on the plate.

The cooked crepes can be stored in a plastic bag and refrigerated for 1 to 2 days, or frozen for 1 to 2 weeks.

# BROWN-BUTTER TART WITH SOUR PLUMS

The brown-butter batter in this tart, or *crostata*, is a very sweet, buttery custard; its sweetness is balanced by an almost savory crust and the extremely sour plums. These small plums vary from yellow to bright red and are available from mid- through late summer. If you can't find them, feel free to use any sour (or even slightly unripe) stone fruit; in the fall and winter, you can substitute fresh cranberries. As the tart bakes, the custard sinks to the bottom and the fruit floats to the top just like pecan pie.

**SERVES 12**

## FILLING

6 ounces (12 tablespoons) unsalted butter

1 vanilla bean, split lengthwise

3 large eggs

1 cup sugar

1½ teaspoons finely grated orange zest

¼ cup unbleached all-purpose flour

½ teaspoon kosher salt

## TART SHELL

4 ounces (8 tablespoons) softened unsalted butter, diced

2 tablespoons sugar

½ teaspoon kosher salt

¼ cup plus 3 tablespoons heavy cream

1 large egg yolk

1½ cups unbleached all-purpose flour

## ASSEMBLY

2½ cups sour plums, pitted and chopped into large dice

Vanilla Gelato (page 204), for serving

**SPECIAL EQUIPMENT**

• 1 (10¼-INCH) TART PAN WITH REMOVABLE BOTTOM

For the filling, heat the butter and vanilla bean in a small saucepan over medium heat. Cook until the butter is a rich, dark brown color, 10 to 15 minutes; the aroma of the brown butter should fill your kitchen. If you are unsure, continue cooking the butter for a few more minutes. Do not be afraid if the bottom of the pan looks almost black—that's a good sign. Remove the pan from the heat. Using a fine-mesh strainer, strain the contents of the pan into a small bowl. Press on the vanilla pod and seeds in the strainer in order to extract all of the delicious vanilla flavor. Set aside the hot butter mixture.

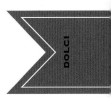

# BROWN-BUTTER TART WITH SOUR PLUMS
## CONTINUED

In a medium bowl, whisk the eggs, sugar, and orange zest. Slowly whisk in the vanilla brown butter and combine until smooth. Add the flour and salt and whisk until smooth. Place the tart filling in an airtight container and let rest in the refrigerator overnight (see Notes). The filling can be made up to 5 days in advance.

For the tart shell, cream the butter, sugar, and salt in a stand mixer fitted with the paddle attachment for 1 to 2 minutes. Add the cream and egg yolk. Mix to combine. Add the flour and beat on low speed just until the dough forms a ball (do not overmix). Wrap the dough in plastic wrap or place in a large resealable plastic bag. Chill for 30 minutes.

Preheat the oven to 350°F. Butter a 10¼-inch tart pan with a removable bottom. On a lightly floured surface, roll out the dough to just over ⅛ inch thick (the diameter will be large enough to fill the tart pan with just a little overhang). Place the rolled dough in the prepared tart pan. Trim off any excess dough on the edges (see Notes). Place a piece of parchment paper or foil over the dough and fill with pie weights or dried beans.

Bake the tart shell for 20 minutes, or until the edges are slightly golden in color. Remove the parchment paper or foil with the pie weights. Continue baking the shell for 10 to 15 minutes longer, until completely golden in color.

To assemble the tart, scatter the plums in an even layer on the bottom of the pre-baked tart shell. Pour the brown-butter batter into the center of the tart. There is no need to spread the brown-butter mixture; it will naturally spread out during the baking process.

Bake the tart until the center no longer jiggles and is slightly puffed up, about 45 minutes. Let cool for 1 hour before removing from the tart pan. Serve with Vanilla Gelato.

**NOTES: Batter:** It's important to let the brown-butter batter rest overnight—this diminishes the air bubbles and gives the batter more uniform consistency.

**Tart shell:** Tart shells often crack during baking, but here's a clever trick to fix them. Save the raw scraps of overhanging dough you trimmed away after placing the dough in the tart pan, and use them to patch the cracks after the shell comes out of the oven. You do not have to rebake the shell.

# OLIVE OIL CAKE WITH CRÈME FRAÎCHE MOUSSE AND RAISIN MARMELLATA

This cake is slightly sweet and incredibly moist, and I almost think it tastes better the day after it is baked. It also has a sturdy, versatile structure—it's my go-to wedding cake recipe, layered up with Italian buttercream. *Marmellata* is Italian for "jam" or "marmalade"; this one features golden raisins lightly poached in a lemony vanilla syrup and spiked with Vin Santo and Grand Marnier. It is perfect next to a slice of olive oil cake or served as a condiment with a platter of Italian cheeses.

## MAKES 1 (9-INCH) CAKE

### CAKE

Nonstick vegetable oil spray

2 large eggs

1¼ cups sugar

¾ cup extra-virgin olive oil

½ cup whole milk

¼ cup Madeira

1¼ cups unbleached all-purpose flour

¼ teaspoon baking soda

¼ teaspoon kosher salt

### MOUSSE

1 cup heavy cream

1 cup crème fraîche

2 tablespoons sugar

### RAISIN MARMELLATA

1 cup golden raisins

3 tablespoons Vin Santo or Madeira (see Note)

Zest and juice of ½ lemon

⅔ cup water

Generous pinch of kosher salt

1 tablespoon Grand Marnier

¼ vanilla bean, split lengthwise

1 cup sugar

Sea salt (preferably Maldon), for garnish

For the cake, preheat the oven to 325°F. Spray a 9-inch cake pan with nonstick spray; line with parchment paper and spray again with nonstick spray. In a large bowl, whisk together the eggs and sugar. Gradually add the olive oil, milk, and Madeira.

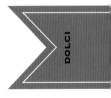

# OLIVE OIL CAKE WITH CRÈME FRAÎCHE MOUSSE AND RAISIN MARMELLATA
**CONTINUED**

In a medium bowl, sift together the flour, baking soda, and salt. Gradually add the dry ingredients to the wet ingredients. Whisk together until smooth, but do not overmix. Pour the batter into the prepared pan. Bake until a wooden skewer comes out clean, 40 to 45 minutes. Let cool for at least 30 minutes before removing from the pan.

For the mousse, whisk the cream, crème fraîche, and sugar in a medium bowl until soft peaks form. Keep refrigerated until ready to serve.

For the raisin *marmellata*, place the raisins in a medium bowl. Set aside. In another medium bowl, combine the Vin Santo, lemon zest, lemon juice, ⅓ cup of the water, the salt, Grand Marnier, and vanilla bean.

Heat the remaining ⅓ cup water and the sugar in a small saucepan over medium-low heat; do not stir. Gradually cook the sugar until it is a medium amber color, 10 to 15 minutes. Slowly swirl the pan to evenly distribute the amber color, wiping down the sides of the pan with a wet pastry brush to dissolve any sugar crystals.

When the caramel reaches the correct medium amber color, remove the caramel from the heat. Slowly add the Vin Santo mixture to the caramel—be careful, as the caramel will rapidly bubble up. Return the saucepan to the heat and slowly stir together the caramel and the liquid. Bring the contents of the pan to a boil.

Pour the caramel mixture over the raisins. Let cool. Serve slightly warm or at room temperature.

To serve, slice wedges of the olive oil cake. Serve each wedge with a generous dollop of crème fraîche mousse and 2 tablespoonfuls of the raisin *marmellata*. Sprinkle sea salt over the mousse to garnish.

**NOTE:** Vin Santo is a traditional Tuscan dessert wine made from dried white grapes. It has a beautiful dark amber color and tastes like nuts, raisins, and honey. This wine is absolutely spectacular and the raisin flavor of the wine is perfect with the raisin *marmellata*. The only drawback is that Vin Santo is relatively expensive. Madeira, a fortified wine from Portugal, is an excellent substitute. Not only does it have a flavor profile and color similar to Vin Santo, but it's easier to find an affordable Madeira.

# BLUEBERRY-POLENTA UPSIDE-DOWN CAKE

Polenta has a million applications in the savory world, but I like to incorporate cornmeal into desserts, too. In this preparation, the cornmeal is added to a brown sugar–buttermilk batter and poured over fresh blueberries. The resulting cake is very moist with a slight crunchy texture from the cornmeal. Be sure to eat the leftovers with coffee for breakfast.

## MAKES 1 (9-INCH) CAKE

### BLUEBERRIES

Nonstick vegetable oil spray

2 ounces (4 tablespoons) unsalted butter

¼ cup light or dark brown sugar

1 vanilla bean, split lengthwise, or 1 teaspoon vanilla extract

2 cups blueberries

### POLENTA BATTER

4 ounces (8 tablespoons) unsalted butter, softened

⅔ cup light or dark brown sugar

½ cup granulated sugar

2 large eggs

1 teaspoon finely grated lemon zest

1 teaspoon vanilla extract

½ cup unbleached all-purpose flour

½ cup fine yellow cornmeal

¾ teaspoon baking soda

¼ teaspoon kosher salt

¼ cup buttermilk

For the blueberries, line a 9 by 2-inch cake pan with parchment paper and spray the bottom and sides with nonstick spray or rub with softened butter.

In a small saucepan, melt the butter and brown sugar over low heat. The mixture may appear separated and that is okay. Remove from the heat and stir in the vanilla bean or vanilla. Pour the butter–brown sugar mixture into the cake pan. Pour the blueberries on top and gently distribute the blueberries all over the bottom of the pan.

For the cake batter, preheat the oven to 325°F. Cream the softened butter, brown sugar, and granulated sugar until light and fluffy. Gradually add the eggs, one at a time, scraping the sides after each addition. Add the lemon zest and vanilla and mix to combine. Sift the flour, cornmeal, baking soda, and salt into a small bowl. Add to the butter mixture. Turn the mixer on low speed and slowly add the buttermilk. Mix on low speed until just combined. If necessary, fold the batter together by hand at the end. Be sure not to overmix the batter.

Pour the batter over the blueberries, using a spatula to evenly distribute the batter. Bake for 45 to 55 minutes, until a wooden skewer comes out clean when inserted into the center of the cake. Remove from the oven and let cool for 20 to 30 minutes. Run a paring knife around the edges of the cake pan. Unmold the cake onto a serving platter. Discard the parchment paper. Remove the vanilla bean pod, if necessary (it will peel off the surface easily). Serve warm or at room temperature.

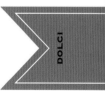

# ESPRESSO-RUM ALMOND CAKE WITH SALTED CARAMEL, SEA SALT GELATO, AND ALMOND BRITTLE

This dessert was a complete accident. I wanted to try out a simple almond cake at dell'anima, but the result was a little dry and a little too crumbly. So I looked around to see what I had on hand. As an experiment, I drowned the cake in espresso and rum and topped it off with sea salt gelato and way too much caramel sauce. It needed a crunch factor; crushed almond brittle was the answer. This recipe went on the menu at dell'anima that night and has remained there ever since. Although there are several components to this recipe, all of them can be made far in advance. In fact, the almond batter can last for several days in the refrigerator before being baked. The cake itself tastes delicious a day or two after it is baked. And the caramel sauce and almond brittle have long shelf lives.

## MAKES 1 (9-INCH) ROUND CAKE

Nonstick vegetable oil spray

4 ounces (8 tablespoons) unsalted butter, at room temperature

1¼ cups sugar

3 large eggs

1 teaspoon vanilla extract

⅔ cup unbleached all-purpose flour

½ teaspoon baking powder

½ teaspoon kosher salt

8 ounces sliced almonds, ground finely

6 ounces almond flour

½ cup milk

2 tablespoons dark or light rum

¼ cup fresh espresso or strong coffee

2 tablespoons simple syrup (see page 12)

Salted Caramel (recipe follows)

Sea Salt Gelato (page 206)

Almond Brittle (recipe follows)

Preheat the oven to 325°F. Spray a 9-inch round cake pan with nonstick spray; line with parchment paper and spray again with nonstick spray.

# ESPRESSO-RUM ALMOND CAKE
**CONTINUED**

In a stand mixer fitted with the paddle attachment, cream the butter and sugar over medium speed, about 2 minutes. Gradually add the eggs and vanilla. Be sure to periodically scrape the sides of the bowl. Add the flour, baking powder, salt, ground almonds, and almond flour. With the mixer running on the lowest speed, gradually pour in the milk. As soon as the batter comes together, remove the bowl from the mixer. With a rubber spatula, scrape the sides of the bowl and fold together until the batter looks homogeneous. Do not overmix the batter. Pour the contents of the bowl into the prepared cake pan. With an offset spatula, smooth the batter into 1 even layer.

Bake for 30 to 35 minutes, until a wooden skewer inserted into the center of the cake comes out clean. Let the cake cool for 30 minutes before removing from the pan.

Stir together the rum, espresso, and simple syrup in a small bowl. With a pastry brush, saturate the top of the almond cake with the espresso mixture. Let sit at room temperature until ready to serve. This cake is very moist and can be made a day in advance. Be sure to store in an airtight container.

Serve each slice of almond cake with warm salted caramel, the sea salt gelato, and a generous sprinkling of almond brittle.

# SALTED CARAMEL

This recipe makes more than you'll need for the cake—which is a good thing, because the sauce is absolutely delicious over almost any dessert or gelato. There are two key tricks to making this caramel sauce. First, make sure that the caramel is a deep dark amber color before adding the cream. You may be nervous about taking the caramel to this stage, but you will be rewarded. The cream will lighten it up and the flavor will remain rich and decadent. Second, don't forget the salt! Caramel is so much better-tasting when it is aggressively seasoned with salt.

**MAKES ABOUT 2½ CUPS**

½ cup water

2 cups sugar

1 cup heavy cream

4 ounces
(8 tablespoons)
cold unsalted
butter, diced

1½ teaspoons sea salt
(preferably Maldon)

Heat the water and sugar over medium-low heat in a medium saucepan; do not stir the contents of the pan. Cook until the sugar starts to turn a light caramel color. Slowly swirl the contents of the pan to distribute the caramel color, wiping down the sides of the pan with a wet pastry brush to dissolve any sugar crystals. Continue cooking the caramel until the color is a very dark amber (if unsure, keep cooking it longer). Slowly add the cream to the caramel—be careful, as the contents of the pan will bubble up ferociously. Whisk the cream and the caramel together. Gradually whisk in the butter, 1 cube at a time. Then whisk in the sea salt. The caramel will be hot, but go ahead and taste it carefully. It should be salty; add more salt if necessary. The caramel sauce can be made several days ahead of time and stored in an airtight container in the refrigerator. To serve warm, reheat the sauce in a small saucepan over low heat or in the microwave on high for about 40 seconds.

## ALMOND BRITTLE

This brittle will last for 3 to 4 weeks at room temperature—if you don't eat it all first. It's a great way to add texture and flavor to any dessert, but it is also delicious sprinkled on Gorgonzola, Taleggio, or any sort of funky washed-rind cheese.

### MAKES 2 CUPS

4 ounces (½ cup) corn syrup

⅓ cup plus 1½ tablespoons sugar

3½ ounces sliced almonds

1 ounce (2 tablespoons) cold unsalted butter, diced

Preheat the oven to 325°F. Line a cookie sheet with a nonstick Silpat liner or with parchment paper.

In a small saucepan, heat the corn syrup and sugar together over low heat. Stir with a heat-resistant spatula until the sugar has melted, 2 to 3 minutes.

Add the almonds and butter. Stir constantly over the heat until the butter has melted and the mixture looks thick with a creamy color; this process only takes a couple of minutes.

Immediately pour the contents of the pan onto the cookie sheet. Using the spatula, spread out the almond mixture so that the almonds are in a single layer. Place the cookie sheet in the oven and bake until the brittle is completely caramelized and has a medium amber color, 35 to 40 minutes. Remove from the oven and let cool on a rack.

When the brittle is completely cool, break it up with your hands into smaller pieces. Place the brittle in a food processor. Pulse until the brittle resembles coarse crumbs. Alternatively, smash the brittle with a rolling pin into smaller pieces. Store in an airtight container at room temperature until ready to serve; the brittle will last 3 to 4 weeks.

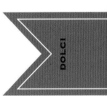

# SICILIAN CANNOLI

Walking between our West Village and East Village restaurants, I can't stop myself from veering into Pasticceria Rocco (better known as Rocco's) on Bleecker Street for a filled-to-order cannoli. But it's also surprisingly easy to make your own cannolis at home. You just need a few pieces of special equipment—metal cannoli dowels and, ideally, a pasta roller—and a little time. The rounds of dough hold well in the freezer and the shells can be fried a day in advance. Be sure not to skimp on the fat content when buying the ricotta; whole milk ricotta will give the cannolis a creamier texture and richer flavor.

---

**MAKES 16 CANNOLIS**

### DOUGH

1¼ cups unbleached all-purpose flour

1 large egg

1 large egg yolk

1 ounce (2 tablespoons) unsalted butter, melted

¼ cup Madeira

½ teaspoon kosher salt

6 cups (48 ounces) vegetable oil, for frying

### FILLING

½ cup heavy cream

2 cups whole milk ricotta

5 tablespoons confectioners' sugar

½ cup finely chopped bittersweet chocolate (70% cacao, preferably Valrhona; see Notes)

1½ tablespoons candied citrus zest (orange and/ or lemon), finely chopped (see Notes)

½ teaspoon kosher salt

3 tablespoons granulated sugar

### ASSEMBLY

Chopped dark chocolate chips

Chopped toasted pistachios

**SPECIAL EQUIPMENT**

• PASTA MACHINE

• 1 (4-INCH) ROUND COOKIE CUTTER

• 6 METAL CANNOLI DOWELS (5½ INCHES BY ¾ INCH)

• PASTRY BAG

For the dough, place the flour, egg, egg yolk, melted butter, Madeira, and salt in a food processor or in a mixer fitted with the paddle attachment. Let the machine run until a dough forms, 1 to 2 minutes. Gather the dough into a ball and wrap tightly in plastic wrap. Let rest in the refrigerator for at least 30 minutes.

# SICILIAN CANNOLI
## CONTINUED

Divide the dough in half. One piece at a time, flour the dough and roll through the thickest setting on a pasta machine. Continue this process, reducing the setting gradually until the dough has completed the second-to-last setting. This is exactly like making pasta. Alternatively, use a rolling pin to roll the dough out on a floured surface to a thickness of 1/8 inch.

Using a 4-inch round cookie cutter, cut each sheet of rolled-out dough into 8 rounds. Place the rounds on parchment paper. As you continue to roll out the dough and cut out the rounds, place a slightly damp cloth over the rounds so that they do not dry out. (The dough rounds can be made ahead and stored in the freezer between layers of parchment paper.)

Pierce the rounds all over with a fork. Roll 6 rounds over the metal cannoli dowels. Place a little water at the end of each round and seal the dough together.

Meanwhile, heat the oil in a large frying pan over medium heat. When the temperature reaches 325°F, use a slotted spoon to lower 3 dough-wrapped cannoli dowels into the oil. Fry for 2 to 3 minutes, until the cannoli shells are golden brown. Remove with the slotted spoon and let cool on paper towels. Add 3 more dough-wrapped cannoli dowels to the oil. When the first 3 shells are cool and the dowels are slightly warm (not hot), use paper towels in each hand to gently remove the shells from the dowels. Continue rolling and frying the cannoli dough rounds in batches of three. The shells can be made a day ahead and stored in an airtight container at room temperature.

For the filling, whip the cream to soft peaks and set aside in the refrigerator.

Place the ricotta, confectioners' sugar, bittersweet chocolate, candied citrus zest, salt, and granulated sugar in a stand mixer fitted with the paddle attachment and mix until well combined, about 2 minutes. Gradually fold the whipped cream into the ricotta mixture. The filling can be made a day ahead and stored in an airtight container in the refrigerator.

To assemble, just before serving, spoon the filling into a pastry bag with a round tip, or into a plastic bag with 1 corner snipped off. Pipe the cannoli filling into the cannoli shells. Dip the ends of the cannoli into either the chopped chocolate or the pistachios to garnish.

**NOTES: Chocolate:** Use whatever brand of bittersweet chocolate you like best. Either chop the chocolate by hand with a chef's knife (I love how the shredded bits of chocolate dissolve into the ricotta filling) or, for a more Italian-American version, substitute mini chocolate chips, which are popular all over Little Italy.

**Candied citrus:** Candied citrus can be found in Italian markets and gourmet stores, but it is easy to make at home. Simply blanch thin strips of citrus zest in boiling water for 2 minutes, then simmer the zest in simple syrup (see page 12) for 5 minutes. Store the candied zest submerged in fresh simple syrup (not the syrup used for cooking). It will keep indefinitely in an airtight container in the refrigerator. When ready to use, drain from the syrup and chop roughly.

# AFFOGATO WITH VANILLA GELATO AND ANISE PIZZELLE COOKIES

The English translation of *affogato* is "drowned," referring to the drowning of gelato in hot espresso. Perhaps this dish should be called *ubriaco* ("drunk") instead: The *affogato* is served with a drunken bath of amaro. Any type of amaro liqueur works well, but so does amaretto, grappa, rum, or Pedro Ximénez sherry. The most important part is to use a freshly pulled, piping hot shot of espresso.

**SERVES 4**

Vanilla Gelato
(page 204)

4 shots of freshly
pulled espresso

4 shots of amaro
(such as Ramazzotti,
Nonino, or Nardini)

4 Anise Pizzelle
Cookies (recipe
follows)

Place a generous scoop of vanilla gelato in each bowl. Pour 1 shot of hot espresso and 1 shot of amaro over each serving. Garnish with the pizzelle cookies. Serve immediately.

## ANISE PIZZELLE COOKIES

I love the crunchy texture and delicate anise flavor of these Italian waffle cookies, which can be flavored with vanilla extract or lemon zest instead.

**MAKES ABOUT 3 DOZEN COOKIES**

1⅓ cups unbleached
all-purpose flour

⅔ cup sugar

2 large eggs

1 tablespoon ground
anise seeds

½ teaspoon kosher salt

4 ounces
(8 tablespoons)
unsalted butter,
melted

Nonstick vegetable
spray, for the
pizzelle maker

**SPECIAL EQUIPMENT**

• PIZZELLE MAKER

Whisk the flour, sugar, eggs, ground anise seeds, salt, and butter in a medium bowl until smooth. Let the batter sit for 1 hour in a covered container. Preheat the pizzelle maker and spray with nonstick vegetable spray, if necessary. When it is hot, add 2 teaspoons to 1 tablespoon of batter to each cookie mold. Cook for 2 to 3 minutes, until golden brown. Remove the cookies and let cool to room temperature. The cookies can be stored in an airtight container at room temperature for several days.

# VANILLA GELATO

Gelato is always best eaten the day that it is spun. But my mom taught me the trick of adding a little vodka to the gelato base. The vodka's high alcohol content prevents the gelato from freezing completely, so it remains creamy and smooth, even a day or two later. And since vodka is flavorless, it does not affect the taste of the gelato.

**MAKES 3 CUPS**

2 cups heavy cream

1 cup whole milk

6 tablespoons sugar

3 vanilla beans, split lengthwise

6 large egg yolks

1½ tablespoons vodka

¼ teaspoon kosher salt

**SPECIAL EQUIPMENT**

• ICE CREAM MAKER

Fill a large bowl with ice water and set aside. Next to the ice bath, place a fine-mesh strainer over a medium metal bowl.

In a medium (3-quart) stainless-steel sauté pan, bring the cream, milk, 3 tablespoons of the sugar, and the vanilla beans to a simmer over medium-low heat. Meanwhile, whisk the egg yolks and the remaining 3 tablespoons sugar in a small bowl.

Slowly add 1 cup of the hot cream mixture to the egg yolks, whisking constantly. (This will temper the eggs so they don't scramble.) Once combined, pour the egg mixture back into the sauté pan and whisk to combine. Place over extremely low heat.

Stirring constantly with a wooden spoon or heat-resistant spatula, gradually cook the cream mixture until a candy thermometer registers 170° to 175°F. At this point, the liquid will be slightly thickened and should coat the back of a spoon.

Immediately pour the cream mixture through the fine-mesh strainer into the metal bowl. (The strainer will remove the vanilla beans and any parts of the sauce that may have curdled during the cooking process.) Using a spatula or spoon, press down on the vanilla beans in the strainer to extract as much flavor as possible. Remove the strainer and place the metal bowl on the ice bath. Stir the vodka and salt into the cream mixture. Continue stirring the custard base until it is cold to the touch. Transfer the custard base to an airtight container with a lid and chill for at least 1 hour or overnight. (The custard base can be prepared 1 to 2 days in advance.)

On the day that you plan to serve the gelato, process the custard base in an ice cream maker according to the manufacturer's instructions. Store the gelato in an airtight container in the freezer until ready to serve.

# CHOCOLATE GELATO

Chocolate gelato should be rich, creamy, and intense with chocolate flavor. This recipe achieves exactly that: Crème anglaise thickened with cocoa powder is poured over bittersweet chocolate. I love the combination of the cocoa flavor combined with the melted chocolate. Be sure to use a high-quality bittersweet chocolate, such as Valrhona.

## MAKES 3 CUPS

4 ounces bittersweet chocolate (70% cacao; preferably Valrhona), finely chopped )

1⅔ cups heavy cream

¾ cup milk

½ cup sugar

8 large egg yolks

1 tablespoon cocoa powder (preferably Valhrona)

¾ teaspoon vanilla extract

¼ teaspoon kosher salt

### SPECIAL EQUIPMENT

• ICE CREAM MAKER

Fill a large bowl with ice water and set aside. Next to the ice bath, place the chopped chocolate in a medium metal bowl and place a fine-mesh strainer over the chocolate.

In a medium (3-quart) stainless-steel saucepan, bring the cream, milk, and ¼ cup of the sugar to a simmer over medium-low heat. Meanwhile, whisk the egg yolks, the remaining ¼ cup sugar, and the cocoa powder in a small bowl.

Slowly add 1 cup of the hot cream mixture to the egg yolks, whisking constantly. (This will temper the eggs so they don't scramble.) Once combined, pour the egg mixture back into the saucepan and whisk to combine. Place over extremely low heat.

Stirring constantly with a wooden spoon or heat-resistant spatula, gradually cook the cream mixture until a candy thermometer registers 170° to 175°F. At this point, the liquid will be slightly thickened and should coat the back of a spoon.

Immediately pour the cream mixture through the fine-mesh strainer into the metal bowl containing the chocolate. (The strainer will remove any parts of the sauce that may have curdled during the cooking process.) Whisk the cream mixture and the chocolate for several minutes to make sure that the chocolate has melted and is thoroughly blended with the cream. Whisk in the vanilla and salt. Place the metal bowl in the ice bath and continue whisking the custard base until it is cold to the touch. Transfer the custard base to an airtight container with a lid and chill the custard base for at least 1 hour or overnight. (The custard base can be prepared 1 to 2 days in advance; cover and keep refrigerated.)

On the day that you plan to serve the gelato, process the custard base in an ice cream maker according to the manufacturer's instructions. Store the gelato in an airtight container in the freezer until ready to serve.

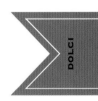

DOLCI

# SEA SALT GELATO

This is a simple gelato base flavored with sea salt. I prefer Maldon salt, which has a great flavor and its saltiness is extremely consistent. But feel free to use any sea salt that you like. Start with half of the amount that the recipe calls for, then taste the base and add more if necessary. A secret I learned in culinary school: Cold foods need more salt than warm foods. This gelato is supposed to taste salty, so don't be shy when seasoning the cold ice cream base.

**MAKES 3 CUPS**

| | | |
|---|---|---|
| 2 cups heavy cream | 6 tablespoons sugar | ½ teaspoon sea salt (preferably Maldon) |
| 1 cup whole milk | 6 large egg yolks | |

**SPECIAL EQUIPMENT**

• ICE CREAM MAKER

Fill a large bowl with ice water and set aside. Next to the ice bath, place a fine-mesh strainer over a medium metal bowl.

In a medium (3-quart) stainless-steel sauté pan, bring the cream, milk, and 3 tablespoons of the sugar to a simmer over medium-low heat. Meanwhile, whisk together the egg yolks and the remaining 3 tablespoons sugar in a medium bowl.

Slowly add the hot cream mixture to the egg yolks, whisking constantly. (This will temper the eggs so they don't scramble.) Once combined, pour the entire mixture back into the sauté pan and place over extremely low heat. Stirring constantly with a wooden spoon or heat resistant spatula, gradually cook the cream mixture until a candy thermometer registers 170° to 175°F. At this point, the liquid will be slightly thickened and should coat the back of a spoon.

Immediately pour the cream mixture through the fine-mesh strainer into the metal bowl. (The strainer will remove any parts of the sauce that may have curdled during the cooking process.) Place the bowl in the ice bath. Stir in the sea salt. Taste the custard. It should be super salty. Feel free to add more salt, if necessary. Continue stirring the custard base until it is cold to the touch. Transfer the custard base to an airtight container with a lid and chill for at least 1 hour or overnight. The base can be prepared 1 to 2 days in advance.

On the day that you plan to serve the gelato, process the custard base in an ice cream maker according to the manufacturer's instructions. Store the gelato in an airtight container in the freezer until ready to serve.

# BANANA-LIME SORBET

Flavored aggressively with lime and spiked with rum, this sorbet has a creamy, smooth texture with a tropical twist. It pairs beautifully with the rice pudding on page 170.

## MAKES 1 QUART

1 cup water

5 tablespoons sugar

2 tablespoons
   corn syrup

Finely grated zest
   of 1 lime

¼ teaspoon kosher salt

4 large bananas

Freshly squeezed
   juice of 1 lime

2 tablespoons dark
   or light rum

**SPECIAL EQUIPMENT**

• ICE CREAM MAKER

In a small saucepan, combine the water, sugar, corn syrup, lime zest, and salt. Place over medium-low heat and cook until the sugar and corn syrup are just dissolved. Strain the mixture through a fine-mesh strainer into the pitcher of a blender. Add the bananas, lime juice, and rum to the blender. Puree the mixture until smooth. Transfer the mixture to an airtight container with a lid and chill thoroughly for several hours or overnight. Process the sorbet in an ice cream maker according to the manufacturer's instructions. Place in a covered container and freeze for 2 to 3 hours before serving.

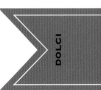

# RASPBERRY SORBET

Refreshing and tart, this raspberry sorbet is a classic. Fresh raspberries are great, but you can also successfully make this sorbet with unsweetened frozen raspberries. The sorbet is excellent served on its own or with the Frutti di Bosco Sundae (page 183); or skip the strawberries and Saba in the crème fraîche panna cotta (see page 177) and serve a scoop of raspberry sorbet alongside instead.

## MAKES 3 CUPS

½ cup water

½ cup sugar

3 cups raspberries, fresh or frozen

1 tablespoon freshly squeezed lemon juice

1 tablespoon light corn syrup

¼ teaspoon kosher salt

**SPECIAL EQUIPMENT**

• ICE CREAM MAKER

Bring the water and sugar to a boil in a small saucepan to make a simple syrup. Remove from the heat.

Place the simple syrup, raspberries, lemon juice, corn syrup, and salt in the pitcher of a blender. Blend to combine, but do not pulverize the raspberry seeds. Pass the mixture through a fine-mesh strainer to remove the seeds. Transfer the mixture to an airtight container with a lid and chill thoroughly.

Process the mixture in an ice cream maker according to the manufacturer's instructions. Store the sorbet in an airtight container in the freezer until ready to serve.

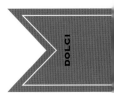

# ROASTED-PINEAPPLE SORBET

Joe's version of the roasted-orange Negroni (see page 2) turned me on to the idea of charring fruit to add a different depth of flavor to a dish. Here pineapples are blackened under the broiler and pureed into a sorbet base. The roasting adds a slight bitterness to the super sweet pineapple and gives the sorbet a caramel color. It might not look like pineapple sorbet, but it definitely tastes like pineapple.

**MAKES 4 CUPS**

2 whole (3- to 3½-pound) pineapples

2 teaspoons finely grated lime zest

2 teaspoons freshly squeezed lime juice

½ teaspoon kosher salt

2 tablespoons corn syrup

½ cup simple syrup (see page 12)

**SPECIAL EQUIPMENT**

• ICE CREAM MAKER

Preheat the broiler to high. Remove and discard the outer layer of the pineapples. Cut the pineapples lengthwise into quarters. Remove and discard the core of each quarter. Place the quarters on a baking sheet and roast until thoroughly charred and blackened on all sides, 10 to 15 minutes per side.

Remove the pineapple quarters from the oven and roughly chop into smaller pieces (you should have about 7 cups). Place the roasted pineapple pieces in a blender. Blend until smooth. Strain through a fine-mesh strainer into a medium bowl, pressing on the pineapple pulp to extract as much juice as possible. Discard the pulp. Rinse out the blender and pour the roasted pineapple juice back into the machine. Add the lime zest and juice, the salt, corn syrup, and simple syrup and blend. Pour into a medium bowl; cover and chill the sorbet base for at least 1 hour or overnight.

Process the sorbet base in an ice cream maker according to the manufacturer's instructions. Store the sorbet in an airtight container in the freezer until ready to serve.

# PEACH PROSECCO SORBET

The Bellini (peach puree with Prosecco) is a world-famous cocktail that originated at Harry's Bar in Venice and is now featured at almost every Italian restaurant. Here is a dessert version of this ubiquitous drink. Fresh peaches—you can use white or yellow; whatever looks good at the market—are poached in an aromatic Prosecco simple syrup, then pureed with the poaching liquid and spiked with Prosecco. The sorbet is a stand-out served by itself. It's also delicious served with fresh raspberries.

## MAKES 5 CUPS

1 (750 ml) bottle Prosecco

2 pounds peaches (about 5 small ripe peaches)

3 cups sugar

½ cup water

1 vanilla bean, split lengthwise

1 bay leaf

1 cinnamon stick

½ cup corn syrup

¾ teaspoon kosher salt

**SPECIAL EQUIPMENT**

• ICE CREAM MAKER

Reserve 1 cup of the Prosecco. To make the peach puree, place the whole peaches, the rest of the bottle of Prosecco, the sugar, water, vanilla bean, bay leaf, and cinnamon stick in a medium (3-quart) saucepan. Place a round of parchment paper over the peaches to keep them submerged. Place over medium-low heat. Bring to a simmer, then decrease the heat to low. Poach the peaches for 25 to 35 minutes, until the peaches are easily pierced with a metal skewer and the skins can easily be removed. (The cooking time will depend on the ripeness of the peaches.) Remove the peaches from the poaching liquid and let cool at room temperature. Strain and reserve the poaching liquid; discard the remaining solids.

Remove the skins and pits from the peaches and discard. Place the peach pulp in a blender and puree until smooth. Measure 3 cups of peach puree (there won't be much more than that) and return to the blender.

To the 3 cups of peach puree, add the corn syrup, salt, 1 cup of the poaching liquid, and the reserved 1 cup of Prosecco. Puree until smooth. Pour the sorbet base into a medium bowl; cover and chill for at least 1 hour or overnight.

On the day that you plan to serve the sorbet, process the sorbet base in an ice cream maker according to the manufacturer's instructions. Store the sorbet in an airtight container in the freezer until ready to serve.

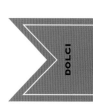

DOLCI

# MACERATED CITRUS WITH PROSECCO SABAYON AND GRAPEFRUIT-APEROL GRANITA

This dessert is light and refreshing—the perfect ending to a heavy winter meal. While navel oranges and grapefruit are available all year round, have fun with the various citrus fruits that appear in the winter months, such as blood oranges and Cara Cara oranges. These fruits each have distinct personalities in terms of sweetness, size, and color. If you would like to serve a cookie alongside, I highly recommend the Semolina Shortbread (page 178).

**SERVES 6**

2½ cups citrus segments (navel oranges, clementines, tangerines, blood oranges, or Cara Cara oranges)

¼ cup plus 2 tablespoons sugar

Freshly squeezed juice of 1 lemon

Generous pinch of kosher salt

4 large egg yolks

⅓ cup Prosecco, Lambrusco Bianco, or any dry sparkling white wine

¼ cup heavy cream

Grapefruit-Aperol Granita (recipe follows)

**SPECIAL EQUIPMENT**

- 6 HIGHBALL GLASSES

In a small bowl, combine the citrus segments, the 2 tablespoons sugar, the lemon juice, and salt. Set aside at room temperature for 30 minutes. The macerated citrus can be made a day ahead of time and stored in a covered container in the refrigerator. Let sit at room temperature for 30 minutes before serving.

To make the sabayon, bring 2 inches of water in a medium saucepan to a simmer. In a large metal bowl, whisk the egg yolks, the ¼ cup sugar, and the Prosecco. Place over the simmering water without letting the bottom of the bowl touch the water. Whisk constantly for 5 minutes, or until the mixture is very thick. The mixture is ready when you can see the bottom of the bowl as you are whisking. Remove from the heat. Let sit at room temperature, whisking occasionally, until the sabayon has cooled.

Meanwhile, place the cream in a small bowl and whisk until the cream forms medium peaks. Fold the whipped cream into the cooled sabayon. Place in a covered container and refrigerate until ready to serve. The sabayon can be made several hours in advance, but it is best served the day you make it.

To serve, distribute the macerated citrus segments among 6 highball glasses. Drizzle each serving with a tablespoon of the macerating liquid. Using an ice cream scoop, place a generous amount of granita on each serving of citrus. Then place a dollop, or quenelle, of sabayon on the granita. Serve immediately.

# GRAPEFRUIT-APEROL GRANITA

Granita is not only easy to make (it does not require an ice cream maker), but also low in calories. In order to give the granita its icy, crystallized texture, the mixture has a lower sugar content than sorbet. This grapefruit version of granita has a beautiful pink color and is unbelievably refreshing served with the macerated citrus and Prosecco sabayon or on its own.

## MAKES 2 CUPS

1¼ cups freshly squeezed grapefruit juice

¼ cup Aperol or Campari

3 tablespoons simple syrup (see page 12)

Pinch of kosher salt

Pour the grapefruit juice, Aperol, and simple syrup into a medium bowl and stir to combine. Season with the salt. Pour into a shallow metal baking pan or container that holds about 1 quart. Cover and place in the freezer overnight or up to 1 week. Use a fork to scrape the frozen grapefruit juice mixture in order to create the granita; serve immediately.

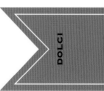
DOLCI

*Chapter 7*

# DIGESTIVI

Though dessert wines can be found in most parts of Italy, *digestivi* are the preferred after-dinner drinks. A *digestivo* is a beverage that you have after dinner because it is thought to aid in digestion. Unlike *aperitivi,* which feature a degree of sweetness or bitterness to help create appetite, *digestivi* are likely to be sweeter or more intensely bitter; they're almost always powerfully strong—putting an exclamation point at the end of a meal.

*Digestivi* are often based on a distilled spirit, sometimes with a flavor infusion. Wine-based *digestivi* are fortified with a spirit. No matter how they're made, we love *digestivi* and feature a huge selection of them at our restaurants, the colorful labels of *amari* and beautiful glass bottles of grappa adorning our bars.

Unlike wine pairings, there are no rules regarding pairing *digestivi* with food—it's entirely personal preference. Personally, I believe bitter *digestivi* are better at aiding digestion; otherwise, it's up to you whether you prefer a strong, sweet, or bitter drink after dinner.

*Strong Digestivi* Once you've had a strong *digestivo,* the appetite is satisfied and the meal is truly finished. Although some brandies (distilled whole fruit spirits) are consumed throughout Italy and whiskey is becoming slightly more popular, **grappa** is the classic strong Italian *digestivo.* Known for its high alcohol content—generally around 40 percent, but sometimes as high as 60 percent, much higher than other *digestivi*—grappa can be intense. But when it's made well, it can be thrilling.

**GRAPPA** is made by distilling pomace—the skins, seeds, stems, and pulp left over after the grapes are pressed during the winemaking process. The type of grape pomace that is used will affect the flavor of the grappa. The vast majority of grappa is clear because it is not aged, but some grappa does have a light brown color due to oak aging. In the past, grappa was a peasant product: It ensured that nothing went to waste and it kept farmers warm through the cold winters. Now artisans are intentionally creating beautiful grappa fit for serving in restaurants and at home.

**THERE ARE FOUR MAIN TYPES OF GRAPPA:**

- Young grappas from non-aromatic grapes (unaged)

- Young grappas from aromatic grapes (grapes like Moscato are very flavorful)

- Cask-conditioned grappas (wood-aged)

- Aromatized grappas (infused with flavors like chamomile and honey)

DIGESTIVI

## OTHER STRONG *DIGESTIVI* INCLUDE:

**GRAPE BRANDIES—**These are mostly made by grappa producers and in wine regions; they tend to be oak-aged and resemble cognac.

**FRUIT BRANDIES—**Made from distilled fruit and produced mostly in the north, these are rare, but can be delicious.

*Sweet Digestivi* Sweet *digestivi* are usually a sweet/strong combination and are often based on fruits or nuts; regional versions can be floral or herb-based.

Sweet and tart, **LIMONCELLO** is an Italian lemon-flavored liqueur produced on the spectacular Amalfi Coast in the south of Italy, where lemon groves cover the terraced hillsides. Grown here since the 1st century, these lemons have adopted the essence of their *terroir* (or "sense of place") and taste vastly different from the industrial lemons we often find in the States; they are sweet and sour in perfect balance. Limoncello has surpassed all other *digestivi* as the most popular liqueur throughout most of Italy, but not all limoncello is created equal; the classic limoncello wears a

DOP (*denominazione di origine protetta*—protected designation of origin). Commonly consumed straight up in a chilled shot glass, limoncello also makes a great mixer. Add limoncello to Prosecco for a refreshing and refined cocktail.

## OTHER SWEET *DIGESTIVI* INCLUDE:

**AMARETTO—**Made from almonds, some versions can be quite sweet. The best have an almost cherry-like natural flavor. I like Luxardo brand.

**NOCINO—**Made from green walnuts harvested in Emilia-Romagna and infused with warming spices, this is a great cold-weather digestivo.

**MIRTO—**Based on the myrtle berry and found in Sardinia, mirto is harder to find, but worth the search. Strong (30% alcohol), it is herbaceously fruity and delicious.

**SAMBUCA—**This is the Italian version of the anise-flavored after-dinner drink found throughout the Mediterranean. I'm not a fan of most Sambucas, as they tend to be very sweet, without the balancing acidity of a dessert wine.

*Bitter Digestivi* These *digestivi* gain their distinct bitterness through the infusion of carminative herbs, which are thought to relieve pressure in the gastrointestinal tract and aid digestion.

**AMARO** (meaning "bitter" in Italian; the plural is amari) is a type of Italian *digestivo* that can range from very dry and bitter to almost syrupy; **AMARI** range between 16 and 35 percent alcohol. Amari are typically produced by macerating herbs, roots, flowers, bark, and/or citrus peels in alcohol (either grape- or grain-based), mixing them with a sugar syrup, and allowing a period of aging in cask or bottle.

A typical *amaro* is flavored with anywhere from 20 to 40 aromatics; some may have as many as 100. Although some ingredients may be named, the full recipes are not divulged and, in fact, are closely guarded secrets. *Amari* are typically flavored with some of the following: gentian, angelica, and cinchona (*china*), lemon verbena (*cedrina*), juniper, anise, fennel, ginger, mint, thyme, sage, bay laurel, citrus peels, licorice, cinnamon, menthol, cardamom, saffron, rue (*ruta*), wormwood (*assenzio*), elder (*sambuco*), and centaurea minor.

There are several different styles of *amari*, with **FERNET** being the most intensely bitter. Due to the success of Fernet-Branca, the most widely imported *amaro*, many people falsely believe that Fernet is a brand. In fact, it is a style. (I like Luxardo brand.) *Amari* are typically drunk neat, with a citrus wedge, on ice, or with tonic water.

*—Joe Campanale*

DIGESTIVI

## ACKNOWLEDGMENTS

There was an incredible team of talented people who were instrumental in putting *Downtown Italian* together. From the editing to the graphic design and photography, it was a true collaboration of ideas, talent, dedication, and plenty of hard work.

First of all, we must thank Andrews McMeel for giving us the creative freedom to publish this cookbook. Kirsty Melville and Jean Lucas helped guide us through the nuances of publishing our first cookbook. They put up with our naïveté and gave us a shot at making our dream cookbook a reality.

It must be said that *Downtown Italian* would not exist without Rosemary Maggiore. From the very beginning, Ro inspired us to make this cookbook. Ro truly believed in the concept and led the project from start to finish. We will forever be grateful to Ro.

Susan Champlin was introduced to us by Kirsty and Jean to edit our manuscript. Susan did that and so much more. Susan peppered us with questions to double-check the measurements and timing of recipes. She noticed mistakes that slipped by us and found words for us when we were going through writer's block. She held us to deadlines and forgave us if we were running behind. Susan even recipe-tested on our behalf. Susan officially went above and beyond her call of duty and we had a blast working with her.

Jill Bluming gets the credit for all of the beautiful pages in *Downtown Italian*. Jill is one of those rare people who reads minds. She met us briefly, visited the restaurants, and put together a gorgeous proposal that was exactly what we had envisioned. Somehow she knew what we wanted. And marrying our words with the graphic design is no small task. Jill is a rock star.

We were also lucky enough to work with the great photographer Tara Donne. Tara and her wonderful team took our recipes and made them come to life. Her talent behind the camera is remarkable. And her willingness to be spontaneous and to push us to think outside the box made each photo shoot memorable.

Also, it was a pleasure to work with the incredible food stylist Chris Lanier. Chris is not only a dear friend, but also encouraged Gabe to pursue a career in cooking and acted as Gabe's mentor for many years. For that and many other reasons, we are indebted to Chris Lanier.

Beyond the book, we have an incredible team of individuals that we work with at the restaurants. These people make it possible for us to work on projects such as this cookbook.

First and foremost, we owe everything to our business partner, August Cardona. August made our dreams come true. He took a huge risk in investing in us when we were relatively young and inexperienced. And he encouraged us to push the boundaries with creativity. Without August's encouragement and savvy business mind, we would not be where we are today.

We must sincerely thank the entire teams, past and present, behind dell'anima, L'Artusi, Anfora, L'Apicio, Epicurean Management, and Epicurean Events. We are spoiled to get to work with so many talented and hard-working individuals. They are responsible for running a smooth ship when we're not there. Because of this crew, we look forward to going to work every single day. But, more importantly, they are our dear friends and family.

Lastly, our families deserve a tremendous amount of thanks. They put up with our stressed-out moments while always acting like our #1 fan club. We would like to thank all of our parents; Ilyssa Satter (Joe's beautiful girlfriend), for being incredibly supportive; Luke Thompson, for eating the food that we recipe-tested; and Emily Thompson, for postponing her delivery until after the book's completion.

*—Joe, Gabe, and Katherine*

# APPENDIX: IL BANCHETTO (THE BANQUET)

## FOUR FEASTS TO CELEBRATE THE SEASONS

### SPRING

**APERITIVI**

Blame It on the Aperol (page 11)

**ANTIPASTI**

Roasted Asparagus with Yogurt and Poached Eggs
(page 68)

**PRIMI**

Orecchiette with Peas and Bacon (page 81)

**SECONDI**

Leg of Lamb with Wilted Spinach and Garlic Confit
(page 145)

**DOLCI**

Frutta al Forno (made with strawberries and rhubarb;
(page 167)

**WINE**

(Rosé) Bonny Doon Vin Gris de Cigare

### SUMMER

**APERITIVI**

Sandia del Fuego (page 9)

**ANTIPASTI**

Summer Squash Salad with Cherry Tomatoes and
Pumpkin Seed Pesto Vinaigrette (page 57)

**PRIMI**

Sweet Corn Mezzaluna (page 97)

**SECONDI**

Roasted Pork Rack with Plums and Chorizo (page 147)

**DOLCI**

Crème Fraîche Panna Cotta with Semolina Shortbread,
Vanilla-Macerated Strawberries, and Saba (page 177)

**WINE**

(White) Foradori Manzoni Bianco

### FALL

**APERITIVI**

The Gilliland (page 25)

**ANTIPASTI**

Tuscan Kale with Roasted-Pear Vinaigrette (page 52)

**PRIMI**

Rigatoni with Roasted Butternut Squash and Bacon
(page 101)

**SECONDI**

Arctic Char with Lentils and Frisée (page 124)

**DOLCI**

Goat Cheese Mousse with Honey-Roasted Figs and
Pine Nut Crisps (page 180)

**WINE**

(Orange) Donkey & Goat Stone Crusher Roussanne

### WINTER

**APERITIVI**

Roasted-Orange Negroni Sbagliatto (page 6)

**ANTIPASTI**

Escarole with Bagna Cauda Dressing and Parmesan
(page 40)

**PRIMI**

Farfalle with Duck Ragù (page 76)

**SECONDI**

Porcini-Rubbed Venison with Roasted Mushrooms and
Walnuts (page 150)

**DOLCI**

Budino di Riso with Caramelized Bananas, Banana-Lime
Sorbet, and Sesame Brittle (page 170)

**WINE**

(Red) Canalicchio di Sopra Brunello di Montalcino

# METRIC CONVERSIONS AND EQUIVALENTS

## APPROXIMATE METRIC EQUIVALENTS

### volume

| | |
|---|---|
| ¼ teaspoon | 1 milliliter |
| ½ teaspoon | 2.5 milliliters |
| ¾ teaspoon | 4 milliliters |
| 1 teaspoon | 5 milliliters |
| 1¼ teaspoons | 6 milliliters |
| 1½ teaspoons | 7.5 milliliters |
| 1¾ teaspoons | 8.5 milliliters |
| 2 teaspoons | 10 milliliters |
| 1 tablespoon (0.5 fluid ounce) | 15 milliliters |
| 2 tablespoons (1 fluid ounce) | 30 milliliters |
| ¼ cup | 60 milliliters |
| ⅓ cup | 80 milliliters |
| ½ cup (4 fluid ounces) | 120 milliliters |
| ⅔ cup | 160 milliliters |
| ¾ cup | 180 milliliters |
| 1 cup (8 fluid ounces) | 240 milliliters |
| 1¼ cups | 300 milliliters |
| 1½ cups (12 fluid ounces) | 360 milliliters |
| 1⅔ cups | 400 milliliters |
| 2 cups (1 pint) | 460 milliliters |
| 3 cups | 700 milliliters |
| 4 cups (1 quart) | 0.95 liter |
| 1 quart plus ¼ cup | 1 liter |
| 4 quarts (1 gallon) | 3.8 liters |

### weight

| | |
|---|---|
| 0.25 ounce | 7 grams |
| 0.5 ounce | 14 grams |
| 0.75 ounce | 21 grams |
| 1 ounce | 28 grams |
| 1.25 ounces | 35 grams |
| 1.5 ounces | 42.5 grams |
| 1.666 ounces | 45 grams |
| 2 ounces | 57 grams |
| 3 ounces | 85 grams |
| 4 ounces (¼ pound) | 113 grams |
| 5 ounces | 142 grams |
| 6 ounces | 170 grams |
| 7 ounces | 198 grams |
| 8 ounces (½ pound) | 227 grams |
| 16 ounces (1 pound) | 454 grams |
| 35.25 ounces (2.2 pounds) | 1 kilogram |

### length

| | |
|---|---|
| ⅛ inch | 3 millimeters |
| ¼ inch | 6 millimeters |
| ½ inch | 1.25 centimeters |
| 1 inch | 2.5 centimeters |
| 2 inches | 5 centimeters |
| 2½ inches | 6 centimeters |
| 4 inches | 10 centimeters |
| 5 inches | 13 centimeters |
| 6 inches | 15.25 centimeters |
| 12 inches (1 foot) | 30 centimeters |

## METRIC CONVERSION FORMULAS

| to convert | multiply |
|---|---|
| Ounces to grams | Ounces by 28.35 |
| Pounds to kilograms | Pounds by 0.454 |
| Teaspoons to milliliters | Teaspoons by 4.93 |
| Tablespoons to milliliters | Tablespoons by 14.79 |
| Fluid ounces to milliliters | Fluid ounces by 29.57 |
| Cups to milliliters | Cups by 236.59 |
| Cups to liters | Cups by 0.236 |
| Pints to liters | Pints by 0.473 |
| Quarts to liters | Quarts by 0.946 |
| Gallons to liters | Gallons by 3.785 |
| Inches to centimeters | Inches by 2.54 |

## OVEN TEMPERATURES

To convert Fahrenheit to Celsius, subtract 32 from Fahrenheit, multiply the result by 5, then divide by 9.

| description | fahrenheit | celsius | british gas mark |
|---|---|---|---|
| Very cool | 200° | 95° | 0 |
| Very cool | 225° | 110° | ¼ |
| Very cool | 250° | 120° | ½ |
| Cool | 275° | 135° | 1 |
| Cool | 300° | 150° | 2 |
| Warm | 325° | 165° | 3 |
| Moderate | 350° | 175° | 4 |
| Moderately hot | 375° | 190° | 5 |
| Fairly hot | 400° | 200° | 6 |
| Hot | 425° | 220° | 7 |
| Very hot | 450° | 230° | 8 |
| Very hot | 475° | 245° | 9 |

### common ingredients and their approximate equivalents

1 cup all-purpose flour = 140 grams
1 stick butter (4 ounces • ½ cup • 8 tablespoons) = 110 grams
1 cup butter (8 ounces • 2 sticks • 16 tablespoons) = 220 grams
1 cup brown sugar, firmly packed = 225 grams
1 cup granulated sugar = 200 grams

Information compiled from a variety of sources, including *Recipes into Type* by Joan Whitman and Dolores Simon (Newton, MA: Biscuit Books, 2000); *The New Food Lover's Companion* by Sharon Tyler Herbst (Hauppauge, NY: Barron's, 1995); and *Rosemary Brown's Big Kitchen Instruction Book* (Kansas City, MO: Andrews McMeel, 1998).

# INDEX